TENANTS' RIGHTS

IN

CALIFORNIA

John J. Talamo
Attorney at Law

SPHINX® PUBLISHING
AN IMPRINT OF SOURCEBOOKS, INC.®
NAPERVILLE, ILLINOIS
www.SphinxLegal.com

First Edition, 2003

Published by: **Sphinx® Publishing, An Imprint of Sourcebooks, Inc.®**

<u>Naperville Office</u>
P.O. Box 4410
Naperville, Illinois 60567-4410
630-961-3900
Fax: 630-961-2168
www.sourcebooks.com
www.SphinxLegal.com

This publication is designed to provide accurate and authoritative information in regard to the subject matter covered. It is sold with the understanding that the publisher is not engaged in rendering legal, accounting, or other professional service. If legal advice or other expert assistance is required, the services of a competent professional person should be sought.

From a Declaration of Principles Jointly Adopted by a Committee of the
American Bar Association and a Committee of Publishers and Associations

This product is not a substitute for legal advice.

Disclaimer required by Texas statutes.

Library of Congress Cataloging-in-Publication Data
Talamo, John.
  Tenants' rights in California / John J. Talamo.
     p. cm.
  ISBN 1-57248-241-9 (pbk : alk. paper)
  1. Landlord and tenant--California--Popular works. 2.
Leases--California--Popular works. I. Title.
KFC145.Z9 T353 2002
346.79404'34--dc21
                                        2002152741

Printed and bound in the United States of America.

VHG Paperback — 10 9 8 7 6 5 4 3 2 1

CONTENTS

USING SELF-HELP LAW BOOKS

Before using a self-help law book, you should realize the advantages and disadvantages of doing your own legal work and understand the challenges and diligence that this requires.

THE GROWING TREND

Rest assured that you won't be the first or only person handling your own legal matter. For example, in some states, more than seventy-five percent of divorces and other cases have at least one party representing him or herself. Because of the high cost of legal services, this is a major trend and many courts are struggling to make it easier for people to represent themselves. However, some courts are not happy with people who do not use attorneys and refuse to help them in any way. For some, the attitude is, "Go to the law library and figure it out for yourself."

We at Sphinx write and publish self-help law books to give people an alternative to the often complicated and confusing legal books found in most law libraries. We have made the explanations of the law as simple and easy to understand as possible. Of course, unlike an attorney advising an individual client, we cannot cover every conceivable possibility.

COST/VALUE ANALYSIS

Whenever you shop for a product or service, you are faced with various levels of quality and price. In deciding what product or service to buy, you make a cost/value analysis on the basis of your willingness to pay and the quality you desire.

When buying a car, you decide whether you want transportation, comfort, status, or sex appeal. Accordingly, you decide among such choices as a Neon, a Lincoln, a Rolls Royce, or a Porsche. Before making a decision, you usually weigh the merits of each option against the cost.

When you get a headache, you can take a pain reliever (such as aspirin) or visit a medical specialist for a neurological examination. Given this choice, most people, of course, take a pain reliever, since it costs only pennies; whereas a medical examination costs hundreds of dollars and takes a lot of time. This is usually a logical choice because it is rare to need anything more than a pain reliever for a headache. But in some cases, a headache may indicate a brain tumor and failing to see a specialist right away can result in complications. Should everyone with a headache go to a specialist? Of course not, but people treating their own illnesses must realize that they are betting on the basis of their cost/value analysis of the situation. They are taking the most logical option.

The same cost/value analysis must be made when deciding to do one's own legal work. Many legal situations are very straight forward, requiring a simple form and no complicated analysis. Anyone with a little intelligence and a book of instructions can handle the matter without outside help.

But there is always the chance that complications are involved that only an attorney would notice. To simplify the law into a book like this, several legal cases often must be condensed into a single sentence or paragraph. Otherwise, the book would be several hundred pages long and too complicated for most people. However, this simplification necessarily leaves out many details and nuances that would apply to special or unusual situations. Also, there are many ways to interpret most legal questions. Your case may come before a judge who disagrees with the analysis of our authors.

Therefore, in deciding to use a self-help law book and to do your own legal work, you must realize that you are making a cost/value analysis. You have decided that the money you will save in doing it yourself outweighs the chance that your case will not turn out to your satisfaction. Most people handling their own simple legal matters never have a problem, but occasionally people find that it ended up costing them more to have an attorney straighten out the situation than it would have if they had hired an attorney in the beginning. Keep this in mind if you decide to handle your own case, and be sure to consult an attorney if you feel you might need further guidance.

LOCAL RULES   The next thing to remember is that a book that covers the law for the entire nation, or even for an entire state, cannot possibly include every procedural difference of every county court. Whenever possible, we provide the exact form needed; however, in some areas, each county, or even each judge, may require unique forms and procedures. In our *state* books, our forms usually cover the majority of counties in the state, or provide examples of the type of form that will be required. In our *national* books, our forms are sometimes even more general in nature but are designed to give a good idea of the type of form that will be needed in most locations. Nonetheless, keep in mind that your *state*, county, or judge may have a requirement, or use a form, that is not included in this book.

You should not necessarily expect to be able to get all of the information and resources you need solely from within the pages of this book. This book will serve as your guide, giving you specific information whenever possible and helping you to find out what else you will need to know. This is just like if you decided to build your own backyard deck. You might purchase a book on how to build decks. However, such a book would not include the building codes and permit requirements of every city, town, county, and township in the nation; nor would it include the lumber, nails, saws, hammers, and other materials and tools you would need to actually build the deck. You would use the book as your guide, and then do some work and research involving such matters as whether you need a permit of some kind, what type and grade of wood are available in your area, whether to use hand tools or power tools, and how to use those tools.

Before using the forms in a book like this, you should check with your court clerk to see if there are any local rules of which you should be aware, or local forms you will need to use. Often, such forms will require the same information as the forms in the book but are merely laid out differently, use slightly different language, or use different color paper so the clerks can easily find them. They will sometimes require additional information.

CHANGES IN THE LAW

Besides being subject to state and local rules and practices, the law is subject to change at any time. The courts and the legislatures of all fifty states are constantly revising the laws. It is possible that while you are reading this book, some aspect of the law is being changed or a court is interpreting a law in a different way. You should always check the most recent statutes, rules and regulations to see what, if any changes have been made.

In most cases, the change will be of minimal significance. A form will be redesigned, additional information will be required, or a waiting period will be extended. As a result, you might need to revise a form, file an extra form, or wait out a longer time period; these types of changes will not usually affect the outcome of your case. On the other hand, sometimes a major part of the law is changed, the entire law in a particular area is rewritten, or a case that was the basis of a central legal point is overruled. In such instances, your entire ability to pursue your case may be impaired.

Again, you should weigh the value of your case against the cost of an attorney and make a decision as to what you believe is in your best interest.

INTRODUCTION

The most valuable asset a landlord can have is a good tenant. Unfortunately, too many landlords do not realize this. They try to cut corners and put short-term gain before the greater value of a good, long-term relationship. What they save by not treating their tenants properly—they lose in turnover and vacancies.

For those who have this type of landlord it is necessary that you know your rights. You must know what to do and how to do it when you are not treated as the law requires.

This is not a book about cheating landlords. You cannot expect good treatment from a landlord that you constantly bother with unfounded complaints and unreasonable demands. The landlord/tenant relationship, like any other relationship, fails in the absence of common sense. Having established the importance of a good relationship, let us move on to how to accomplish it.

You have probably bought this book for one of three reasons. You are going to rent a place to live and want advice to help you find the best place on the most favorable terms. The second reason is that you are already renting a unit and are having problems with your landlord, roommate, or other tenants. The third situation is that you want to leave your rental unit and are afraid you may suffer some financial loss by breaking a lease or failing to get back your security deposit.

This book covers each of these three main areas. Chapters 1 and 2 will help you find the right place for you and avoid an unfavorable lease or rental agreement. Chapters 3 through 12 concern your rights as a tenant, such as your right to privacy and maintenance of your unit. Chapters 12 through 15 are about leaving the unit, whether voluntarily or under the threat of eviction.

This book also discusses special issues for tenants to consider. Chapter 16 gives you valuable information about what tenants' organizations have to offer. Chapter 17 tells you how to acquire and live with roomates and lodgers. Finally, Chapter 18 explains rules and gives advice for using self-storage.

FINDING A PLACE TO RENT 1

As with most things of importance that you do, research and preparation produce a favorable result. There are several things you must consider before you start your search.

RENT

Decide how much rent you can realistically afford. This sounds easy, but many people do not stick to this amount. They see a place they really like and agree to pay more than they originally planned. Many times it turns out to be more than they can afford.

Rent should include utilities and all costs associated with the location. In other words if you have to take a toll road to work from your new place which adds $100/month to your budget, that is part of your rent. If your children have to now pay for school or a bus to get them there, that is part of your rent. Any increase in your expenses caused by your new location is part of your rent.

This is not the usual way people go about figuring rent but it puts things into perspective. If you had planned to pay $1000/month and after adding all associated costs, you are paying $1500, you may want to consider another place.

Rent changes, almost always upward. How often and how much it changes varies. When doing your research, you should try to determine how often the rent increases and the amount of the usual increase. Ask the landlord or manager and, if possible, ask other tenants.

Also, find out how long the current owner has owned the property and whether new improvements have just taken place or are planned. A new owner planning improvements will almost certainly increase the rent when they are completed.

SPACE

The number and size of rooms has to be carefully considered. You do not want to pay for space you do not need; however, you want to live comfortably. Measure your larger pieces of furniture, such as beds and couches. Make a list of all your furniture and mentally arrange your prospective unit as you look through it. The number of people who need to get ready at the same time for work or school should give you an idea of the number of bathrooms you need.

This, of course, does not apply to everyone. You may already know your needs. However, if you are expanding the number of people you will be living with (new spouse with children, roommates, etc.), this may be critical.

Always bring a tape measure and pad and pencil with you when looking at a unit. Write down room sizes if you are unsure whether your furniture will fit and make notes of any damage to the unit. It is not necessary to take pictures at this time but you should ask if any repairs or improvements (carpet, paint, drapes, etc.) will be made. A checklist is provided in Chapter 19.

Additional storage space and parking are also important. Do you have assigned parking or are you going to have a long walk to your car most days (sometimes in inclement weather)? If there is additional storage space, how large and convenient is it?

Finally, if you are looking in an apartment complex, drive through the parking area in the early evening. Take a look at the cars parked there. You will get some idea of how the tenants take care of their belongings. Also, if the weather is good, you may see people hanging around the carports (usually a sign of overcrowding in the units).

TIME OF OCCUPANCY

How long you plan to stay in the unit will affect both rent and space. If you need a place for a few months while your new house is being built or your job transfer comes through, you might decide to pay a little more and be comfortable or take less space and save some money. Either way, it will not matter for very long. However, if there is a good chance that you may be in the unit for a long period of time, both rent and space become more important.

The amount of space you need may also change. The amount of space you have will not. Is one of your children getting ready to move out soon or is your child having marital problems and about to move back in?

You may not always be able to predict your needs. If you are in an apartment complex, ask the landlord or manager about other rental units (larger or smaller) that you may want in the future. This is especially important if you are going to commit to a lease. You may be able to include a clause in the lease that will allow you to change units without any breach of your agreement.

LOCATION

Where you rent is, of course, dependent on your lifestyle and ability to pay. Again, a list is helpful. Write down the things most important to you. Then try to create a balance (you probably will not be able to get them all). Is it more important to be close to a school or close to a church? If you have small children, perhaps the school. If you have one teenager who drives and you are involved in church activities, perhaps the church. Do you enjoy taking walks? Will you be able to do that in your new neighborhood? How close will you be to water (a beach, river, or lake)?

There is also the obvious consideration of commuting to work. There are many places that offer lower rents if you are willing to commute. Let us say you work in Los Angeles. If you are willing to drive from Riverside or San Bernardino, you can get a larger unit for less rent.

There are three things to consider. First, add the additional cost of the commute. The extra cost of toll roads, gas and wear and tear on your car may negate the savings on rent. Second, the aggravation may not be worth the savings. You may want to try the drive a few times to get an idea of how much you can take. The third consideration is time. Spending two or more hours in traffic every day may take so much enjoyment out of your life that the commute is just not worth it.

SAFETY

Safety is always a concern. There are several things you should check. Drive through the neighborhood at different times of the day. If you see joggers and people strolling, you know that at least some people consider it safe.

Ask the landlord about safety at the building and in the area. Does the building have special security? Why? Is it just a precaution or because there have been problems? Talk to current tenants if possible.

Visit the local police precinct or sheriff's office. Ask specifically about problems at your building as well as general information about the area.

Also ask to use the computer to check registered sex offenders. This can be done by zip code and will give you more information about possible problems. There is no cost for this but you will have to fill out a short form and state that you are not a sex offender. More information on checking for registered sex offenders in your county can be found at:

http://caag.state.ca.us/megan/info.htm

PREPARATION

A typical TENANT APPLICATION is provided in Appendix C. There is no standard application used for all rental units, but this one will give you a good idea of the information you will be asked to provide. Having the information available will allow you to fill out the application on the spot rather than having to take it home and send it back. If several people are interested in the same unit, this could make the difference between getting it and being too late.

CREDIT REPORTS

It is common today for a landlord to run a credit check on a prospective tenant. Credit bureaus make mistakes and you may not have the good credit that you think you have. For a small fee you can get your credit report from a credit bureau or a company that will get it for you. This can be done by phone or online.

Once you get the report, make several copies. Attach one to each rental application you fill out. Landlords are allowed to charge a fee to check your credit. This could save you the fee and speed up the process. If the landlord still wants to check your credit, ask if the fee will be returned if you do not get the unit. (You will be asked for the fee up front.)

If your credit report is incorrect, you will have a chance to correct it. You do not want to wait until you get a letter from the landlord stating that you have been turned down for bad credit. By the time you correct the report, the unit will most likely be rented to someone else.

Leases and Rental Agreements 2

A lease or rental agreement is a contract. What is a *contract*? Simply put, if you give your word (orally or in writing) and the law says you must keep it, you have made a contract. There are many rules that govern when you must keep your word but the main thing to remember is that you should not agree to anything with the landlord that you do not want to do or you believe is unfair.

Leases exceeding one year must be in writing to be enforceable. Verbal leases are enforceable if for a term of a year or less, but this is rarely done. Chances are you will have to sign a lease or rental agreement.

The difference between a *lease* and a *rental agreement* is simple. If there is a definite time period for the rental, it is a lease. It does not matter if the time period is one week or ten years. If there is no definite time limit but only a set time when rent is paid, it is a rental agreement.

Most units require a rental agreement with rent paid monthly. This means that you can move out at any time (without giving a reason) after proper notice and not be liable for future rent. If rent is paid monthly, thirty days would be proper notice.

However, if you sign a lease, you cannot move out until the lease expires unless you have a "legal excuse." You can, of course, always move out, but you may be liable for future rent until the end of the lease. This is what is known as *breach of contract*. This will also be discussed in detail in Chapter 13.

The safe way to think about a lease when you first enter into it is that you will be bound by all its provisions. If there is something in it that you do not like or do not completely understand, do not sign it until you are satisfied that you can live with it.

Unlike some other contracts, leases do not have a *recision period*. Once you sign it there is no grace period during which to avoid the agreement simply because you changed your mind.

Typical leases for both apartments and condominiums and a common rental agreement are provided in Appendix C. There is no standard lease or rental agreement that all landlords use, but these samples will cover most situations. Read the appropriate one for your situation carefully along with the explanations of some of the clauses to be sure you understand all the provisions.

There are also special agreements that you may be asked to sign in addition to your lease. This may be because the lease does not cover these areas or because the landlord wants a more specific understanding than the lease covers. A typical example would be a PET AGREEMENT. These agreements will refer to the lease and become part of it.

The following chapters will deal with the most important parts of the lease in more detail, as well as these additional agreements.

DISCRIMINATION 3

Discrimination in the sale or rental of property has been addressed by the federal government as early as 1866, when it passed the Civil Rights Act, Section 1982, applying only where it can be proved that the person intended to discriminate. The statute states that "all citizens of the United States shall have the same right, in every State and Territory, as is enjoyed by white citizens thereof to inherit, purchase, lease, sell, hold, and convey real and personal property."

Over 100 years later in 1968, Congress clarified its ban on housing discrimination by passing the Fair Housing Act (FHA), which is Title VIII of the above mentioned Civil Rights Act. The Fair Housing Act makes it a federal crime for a landlord to discriminate in the rental or sale of property on the basis of race, religion, sex, or national origin. In addition, California has passed its own anti-discrimination statute, called the Fair Employment and Housing Act The California act mirrors the federal act, and may be accessed at the California Department of Fair Employment and Housing website at **www.dfeh.ca.gov**.

Congress then went even further with the FHA Amendment Acts of 1988, which incorporates and expands the earlier acts and sets out the rules and penalties for discriminating.

CIVIL RIGHTS ACT, SECTION 1982

PENALTIES FOR
DISCRIMINATION

As penalty, the landlord must pay actual damages plus unlimited punitive damages. *Actual damages* are the amount of money that the plaintiff lost because of the defendant's wrongdoing. *Punitive damages*, also called *exemplary damages*, are meant to punish the defendant and set an example meant to deter future wrongdoing both from the defendant and others. They are usually awarded when the violation is intentional and especially offensive.

Example: If a landlord were to tell you that he does not rent to people of your race or religion, you might lose money by having to rent a similar unit elsewhere at a higher rent. This would be your actual damages. Since the violation was obviously intentional and offensive, a jury would also most likely award punitive damages. While your actual damages might be only a few hundred dollars, the punitive damages could be hundreds of thousands or more.

Of course, few landlords are so blatant, but if the jury believed the reason for the refusal to rent was based on racial or religious bias, the result would be the same.

FAIR HOUSING ACT

Under the Fair Housing Act, any policy that has a discriminatory effect is illegal. Failure to attend a hearing or to produce records can subject a landlord to up to a year in prison or a $1,000 fine. (United States Code, Title 42, Sections 3601 to 3619.)

FILING A
DISCRIMINATION
SUIT

A victim of discrimination under this section can file a civil suit, a HUD complaint, or request the U.S. Attorney General to prosecute. Damages can include actual losses and punitive damages of up to $1,000.

If you believe that you have been discriminated against, consult a lawyer. Bringing the suit under one act rather than another can make a difference in the award you receive. The complaint must be brought within 180 days.

EXEMPTIONS This law does not apply to single family homes if:

- the landlord owns three or less homes;

- there is no more than one sale within twenty-four months;

- the person does not have an ownership interest in more than three homes at one time; and,

- no real estate agent or discriminatory advertisement is used.

It also does not apply to a property that the owner lives in if it has four or fewer units.

Where coercion or intimidation is used to effectuate discrimination, there is no limit to when the action can be brought or the amount of damages.

Example: The landlord tells the prospective tenant that she will be the only tenant in the building with children and if her children cause even the slightest problem, she will be evicted.

FAIR HOUSING ACT 1988 AMENDMENT

The 1988 Amendment to the Civil Rights Act bans discrimination against the handicapped, the elderly, and families with children. (United States Code, Title 42, Section 3601.)

Unless a property falls into one of the exemptions, it is illegal under this law to refuse to rent to persons because of age or to refuse to rent to families with children. While some landlords may feel that children cause damage to their property that they wish to avoid, Congress has ruled that the right of families to find housing is more important.

The law applies to two types of housing:

- where units are rented solely by persons sixty-two or older, or

- where eighty percent of the units are rented to persons fifty-five or older.

In late 1995, the law was amended so that the property does not need special facilities for such persons' needs. If you are disabled, the law allows you to remodel the unit to suit your special needs as long as you return it to the original condition upon leaving. It also requires new buildings of four units or more to have electrical facilities and common areas accessible to the disabled.

PENALTIES   If a landlord is convicted of refusing to rent to persons because of age, disability, or because they are a family with children, he or she will pay steep penalties. A landlord must pay $10,000 for the first offense, $25,000 for the second violation within five years, and up to $50,000 for three or more violations within seven years. There are unlimited punitive damages in private actions.

The complaint must be brought within two years for private actions.

EXEMPTIONS   This law does not apply to single family homes if:

- the landlord owns three or less homes;

- there is no more than one sale within twenty-four months;

- the person does not own any interest in more than three at one time; and,

- if no real estate agent or discriminatory advertisement is used.

NOTE: *A condominium unit is not a single-family home, so it is not exempt.*

It also does not apply to property that the landlord lives in if it has four or fewer units.

ADDITIONAL
EXEMPTIONS

The law does not apply to:

- dwellings in state and federal programs for the elderly;

- complexes that are solely used by persons sixty-two or older; and,

- complexes used solely by persons fifty-five or over, if there are substantial facilities designed for the elderly, for religious housing, and for private clubs.

CALIFORNIA LAWS

The most comprehensive law is California Civil Code, Section 51, known as the Unruh Act, which prohibits discrimination on the basis of race, religion, national origin, ethnic background, gender, marital status, age, disability, sexual orientation, income from government assistance, personal traits, and families with children.

DISCRIMINATION
VERSUS EQUAL
TREATMENT

Discrimination can take place at any time during the rental process. This includes advertising, negotiating the agreement, after the tenant moves in (raising the rent or security deposit, for example), and eviction.

Does this mean that your rent cannot be raised? No. It means that all tenants should be treated equally. Raising only your rent while others with the same facilities do not get the increase can be considered discrimination. There would be an exception if, for example, improvements were made to your unit only.

A few common sense things to remember are:

- All applicants and tenants should be treated equally.

- Approximately the same rent and security deposit should be charged for all similar units.

- Rents and security deposits should be raised equally. There can be some variation based on how long the unit has been occupied. If the landlord raises rents after one year of occupancy, this could create different rents without discrimination. In fact it could be discrimination to raise one tenant's rent after, say, one month and another's after one year, even though the rents were the same.

- A landlord should not evict one tenant for something that was ignored when done by another tenant.

If you are refused rental because of your age, be sure it is because you are too young. California *allows* discrimination based on age by allowing senior citizen only housing. (California Civil Code, sections 51.3 and 51.4.)

DRUG ADDICTED TENANT

A landlord cannot refuse to rent to a person convicted of drug use or possession. Drug addiction is considered a disability. Do not confuse this with drug dealing. A conviction for the manufacture or sale of drugs would be a legitimate reason to refuse to rent. A landlord must act to stop drug dealing, typically by eviction, or be subject to liability. If you know of a tenant manufacturing or dealing drugs in the building that you rent, informing the landlord requires him to take action (at least to look into your claim to determine its truth.)

U.S. DEPARTMENT OF HOUSING AND URBAN DEVELOPMENT (HUD)

The U.S. Department of Housing and Urban Development (HUD) is responsible for administering all laws related to housing discrimination. Contact California's HUD for more information about these laws at:

HUD
450 Golden Gate Ave.
San Francisco, CA 94102
415-436-6550
800-343-3442
or
www.hud.gov

SECURITY DEPOSITS 4

A security deposit is important to you at two different times. The first is when you are moving in and have to pay the deposit. The second is when you are moving out and want to get it back.

The law regarding security deposits is controlled by the California Civil Code, Section 1950.5. It applies to rentals that are longer than thirty days, but not to short term rentals such as hotels, motels, and vacation homes.

AMOUNT

Under this law, any money given to the landlord by the tenant above the normal rent is considered a refundable *security deposit*. It does not matter if it is called non-refundable, a cleaning fee, moving in fee, last month's rent or a larger first month's rent payment. Any amount paid at the beginning of the tenancy that is above one month's rent is considered a security deposit and must comply with the law.

The maximum amount allowed is two months' rent for an unfurnished unit and three months' rent for a furnished unit. A tenant with a pet may be charged a larger deposit than a tenant without a pet without liability for discrimination, but in either case, the amount may not exceed the two or three months limit. A tenant with a waterbed may be charged a maximum of one-half month's rent over the amounts stated above. Pets and waterbeds are discussed in more detail in Chapter 5.

Under a month to month rental agreement, a landlord cannot collect advance rent payments above the security deposit amount allowed by law. In other words, a landlord cannot collect six months prepaid rent. The maximum amount would be four months (first month's rent plus three months security deposit for a furnished unit). This is true even if the landlord is going to credit you each month with the rent payment and deduct the amount from the prepaid rent. However, if you have a lease of six months or longer, the landlord may collect prepaid rent in addition to the maximum amount of the security deposit allowed.

Although California law does not require interest to be paid on security deposits, some cities have local ordinances that require it. Ask the landlord if this applies to your location. If the answer is no and you do not believe it, check with the city.

PICTURES

It is important that you photograph your rental unit both before you move in and when you are moving out. You can bet that the landlord will also do this. Photos from different angles may show the same subject differently. The landlord will show the pictures most favorable to his argument. You should be able to do the same.

On the pictures you take when you move in, write the date, the room photographed, and the damage you see when taking the picture.

Example: Feb. 7, 2003, bathroom off master bedroom, two-inch crack on left side of medicine cabinet.

If you are not using an instant camera, write this information on a piece of paper with the number of the picture displayed by the camera. Transfer this information to the back of the picture when you get it developed. When you move out, do the same. This will give you a realistic assessment of any damages you may be responsible for as well as protection from a landlord's unjust claims.

KEEPING THE DEPOSIT

California Civil Code, Section 1950.5, allows a landlord to deduct only the following items from the security deposit:

- unpaid rent;

- repair for damages caused by the tenant, tenant's guest, or licensee, exclusive of normal wear and tear;

- cleaning after the tenant leaves; and,

- return of personal property or appurtenances if the security deposit agreement calls for it.

The landlord may deduct damages from a security deposit, but may not deduct normal wear and tear. The difference is a question of fact that only a judge or jury can decide using a *standard of reasonableness*. A hole in a wall is clearly not reasonable. An apartment that needs painting after you have lived there ten years is just as obviously reasonable. Between those two extremes you have to use common sense. If you feel that the landlord has deducted something that should not be deducted, contact the landlord first. If you are not satisfied, you can sue in small claims court. If you decide to do this, you should show your before-and-after pictures to others in order to verify your judgment before showing them to the judge.

LIQUIDATED DAMAGES CLAUSE

If you are signing a lease (meaning there is a definite date when your tenancy ends), beware of a "Liquidated Damages" clause. This is a clause that allows a landlord to keep the entire deposit or a portion of it if you leave before the lease is up (breach your contract). *Liquidated damages* are simply an agreed upon amount of damages if there is a breach, and they are legal. What is not legal is a penalty. A court decides whether the clause is a liquidated damages clause *or* a penalty. Since the controlling factor is what is "reasonable," you can not really know the answer except in extreme cases.

STATEMENT OF
DEDUCTIONS

In order to make deductions from your security deposit the landlord must send you an itemized statement of the deductions. This must consist of the amounts that the landlord intends to keep and the reasons for keeping these amounts.

Example: $50 to replace a medicine cabinet that has a crack caused by the tenant that cannot be repaired. Sound familiar? It is probably the one you took the picture of when you first moved in, saving you $50.

This itemized statement must be mailed to your last known address no later than three weeks after you vacate the property. This applies even if you are evicted and owe rent that exceeds the deposit. If you did not give the landlord a forwarding address, you will still get the statement as long as you filed a change of address with the post office. The landlord will send the statement to the address you just left.

NOTE: *If the landlord claims things that are not legitimate, the court can assess a penalty of up to $600 in addition to forcing the return of the deposit. An* ITEMIZED SECURITY DEPOSIT DISPOSITION *form is included in this book as form 20 so that you can familiarize yourself with it before you actually get one.*

If the landlord writes on the check "Accepted in full payment of claims against security deposit," and it is not the amount you should receive, either accept the check and take your loss (the check could be off by fifty cents) or do not cash it and file suit.

WHEN PROPERTY IS SOLD

If you damage your living area, you lessen the value of the property. The new owner will want to pay less because of this. The current owner will charge your security deposit to make up for this price reduction or to make repairs before the sale is final.

SECURITY DEPOSIT CHARGED	This means that your security deposit may be charged at this time even though you still occupy the property. You will have an unexpected expense. To prevent this, it is a good idea to repair anything you have damaged in a timely manner, rather than waiting until you are ready to move out. This, of course, applies only to those things you are responsible to repair.
SECURITY DEPOSIT INCREASED	Another situation that often occurs when a property is sold is that security deposits are raised. Landlords usually do not raise your security deposit when they raise your rent, even though it would be legal to do so. However, a new owner will often raise the security deposits to reflect current rents or to the maximum legal amounts. This is especially true if the new owner makes improvements to the property. If you are on a tight budget, it is wise to keep some money put aside for this possibility. If you have a lease (rather than a rental agreement) with a fixed rent and security deposit, it can not be raised.

A buyer of the property may ask you to verify the amount of the deposit before closing the purchase to verify the amount given by the seller. It's okay to do this. Just make sure that that is *all* you are doing.

SPECIAL AGREEMENTS 5

This chapter covers special situations, such as insurance related to dealing with someone in addition to your landlord (insurance agent) as well as those situations where you may be asked to sign a document in addition to your lease, such as a pet or water bed agreement.

INSURANCE

Insurance can cover a multitude of potential problems. You should carry *tenant's insurance* to protect against damage to or theft of your furniture and personal belongings. If you call an insurance agent and ask for *renter's insurance*, it will cover theft and damage to your personal property, as well as liability. You need liability insurance to protect you if you are responsible for injury or damage to someone else's person or property. You should always go over the amounts with your insurance agent to be sure they are sufficient to protect your property and protect you against liability. Landlords may demand that you carry tenant's insurance.

RIDER   If you have needs beyond the normal coverage, you can buy additional insurance. You may have a diamond ring, for example, that is worth more than the normal coverage. You can cover it with a separate policy or what is called a *rider* to the usual tenant's policy. This will also cover any deductible (portion of the damage or theft not covered) in the general policy.

It is also a good time to tell your agent if you have a pet or water bed. If your agent says that your breed of dog cannot be covered or your water bed does not meet industry standards, you can deal with the problem before your landlord is aware of it.

Contact your agent as far in advance as possible. This gives you two advantages. First, you can shop around for insurance. Second, when you apply for the rental, you can tell the landlord that your water bed, for example, is insurable. Do not volunteer this information if you are not asked.

PETS

Landlords have the right to prohibit pets or restrict the type of pets allowed unless they are necessary for a disabled tenant, such as a seeing-eye dog. For this reason you should always get permission in writing for your specific type of pet.

You should also get insurance to cover possible damage from having the pet. There is the obvious dog bite problem, but a large bird may also cause serious injury. A tropical fish tank could leak or break. Check with your insurance agent for all the proper protection.

If you have a dangerous or wild animal, a landlord is foolish to rent to you. The landlord could be liable for injury caused by your boa constrictor, for example. It will also be difficult to get insurance. Most insurance companies are even refusing to cover certain breeds of dogs, such as pit bulls. This is true even if the dog has shown no past aggressive tendencies.

The pet agreement that you will be asked to sign becomes part of your lease or rental agreement. It will most likely specify the animal(s) that you can keep on the property and a description of "unacceptable behavior" by the animal. This behavior will be grounds for eviction with a three-day notice. In addition it will contain an *indemnity clause*. This means that not only are you liable for suits against you from your animal's causing damage or injury, but you agree to pay for any of the landlord's financial loss if he gets sued. A typical **PET AGREEMENT** is provided in Appendix C.

NOTE: *If you are renting a house, you may want to put a "beware of dog" sign out. Some people think it's clever to put out signs like "Trespassers will be eaten." Some insurance companies say that this shows that you know the dog is vicious and refuse to cover an injury caused by the dog. It also could be used against you by the person suing for the damages caused by the dog. A sign like "Dog on the property. Don't open gate" gets the idea across without any admissions. The sign could be there so no one accidentally lets the dog out of the yard to get lost or hit by a car.*

WATER BEDS

If you are renting in a fairly new building, you are allowed to have a water bed. California Civil Code Section 1940.5 states that the landlord may not prohibit a water bed if the building's certificate of occupancy was issued after January 1, 1973.

However, your security deposit may be increased up to an additional one half month's rent. The landlord can require that you obtain insurance against the possible damage and that the bed conforms to industry standards. If there is a problem, check with the people who sold you the bed. Your insurance agent should also be able to help. If the bed is insurable, the landlord usually does not quibble about industry standards.

CHANGING THE TERMS OF THE TENANCY 6

The landlord/tenant relationship is no different from any other contractual relationship. The original situation may change, requiring a change in the agreement between the parties. This can be as simple as your landlord raising the rent or it can be more complicated, such as your leaving before the lease expires and wanting someone else to take over your obligations. The ability to change the original terms of the tenancy will be governed by the agreement between the parties (lease or rental agreement) and by the requirements of the law.

ASSIGNMENT OR SUBLEASE BY TENANT

You may desire to turn over all or part of the premises to a third party. This can be done in one of two ways: an assignment or a sublease.

An *assignment* is where you transfer all of your interest in a lease to another party, who takes over your position. The new tenant takes your place and deals directly with the landlord. The new tenant pays rent directly to the landlord.

A *sublease* is where you lease all or part of the property to a third party. This new party (called a *subtenant* or *sublessee*) is responsible to you (called the *sublessor*). You are still responsible to the landlord. The sublessee pays her rent to you (the sublessor), and you then pay the rent to the landlord.

LANDLORD'S
DUTY TO
MITIGATE

Subleases and assignments are allowed unless prohibited by the terms of the lease. However, even if prohibited by the lease, California law places a *duty to mitigate* on the landlord. This means that a landlord has a duty to make reasonable efforts to rent the property in the event the tenant leaves before the end of the lease term. If you offer your landlord a new tenant who is reasonably acceptable, he cannot refuse her and still hold you liable for rent for the balance of the lease term.

The usual terminology in a lease agreement requires the landlord's written consent for a sublease or assignment. This allows the landlord to screen the proposed new tenant before deciding whether to allow the sublease or assignment. You should approach subleasing and assignment from the landlord's point of view. Do a little preliminary work on your proposed new tenant. I advise that you check her credit as well as her job status. You are only wasting your time if you submit someone who you would not rent to if you were the landlord.

Once you have determined that your tenant is responsible enough to take over your lease, submit the request to the landlord in writing. Attach a copy of the credit report and a tenant application. This lets the landlord know that you know what you are doing as well as speeds up the process. As with any writing, keep copies of everything you submit and be sure to date the request.

NOTE: *Submitting things in writing usually gets you a written answer. Verbal requests usually get a verbal response. Getting things in writing is better for everyone concerned.*

LANDLORD'S
CONCERN

There are two ways that the landlord can give consent to accept the new tenant. They are called *express* and *implied*. *Express consent* simply means that words are used to give the consent, whether written or verbal. This is normally what we think of as giving consent. The law also says that if your actions show that you agree, you have given consent even though no words were used. This is called *implied consent*. If the landlord accepts rent from the new tenant, for example, it may show that the landlord agreed to accept the new tenant, even though he never said (or wrote) that he accepted her.

NEW TENANT'S
RENT

Get your proposed tenant to give the landlord the next rent check. Do this even if you actually pay the rent by reimbursing your new tenant because she has not moved in yet. Have a notation on the check, such as "February rent for unit 8" or the property address and unit number if the landlord has other property or you are paying a management company. The landlord may not realize the implications of accepting the check, but the landlord's lawyer will if there is a later dispute.

If more people are now going to occupy the unit, the landlord may raise the rent and security deposit. You and the new adult occupant(s) may be asked to sign a new lease or you may receive a thirty-day notice if you have a rental agreement. Of course, if you are no longer going to occupy the property, you will not sign the new agreement.

If the rent or security deposit increases, check rent control laws (if applicable to your property) to make sure the increase does not exceed the maximum allowed. The security deposit cannot be increased beyond the maximum (two months rent for unfurnished, three months for furnished) even if the property is not covered by rent control.

NOTE: *If the landlord raises the rent by a notice rather than by a new lease, you must be given 60 days notice if the increase is more than ten percent in one year.*

SALE OF PROPERTY BY LANDLORD

A landlord has the right to sell property covered by a lease, but the new owner takes the property subject to the terms of any existing lease. The new owner cannot cancel the old lease or raise the rent while the lease is still in effect (unless the lease has provisions allowing this).

Your mere occupancy of the unit gives the new owner the obligation to investigate your situation. In other words, the new owner cannot say that he is not bound by a lease because the old owner said you did not have one.

NOTICE

This is about what the law calls *notice*. You do not hold the new owner responsible for things he does not know exist, such as your lease. However, the law creates a *duty to inquire*. This prevents deliberate ignorance by the new owner. The fact that you occupy the unit means that there may be a lease. This creates a duty on the part of the new owner to find out if there is a lease. If the new owner chooses not to inquire, he will still be bound by the terms of your lease.

However, verbal agreements with the old owner may be in jeopardy. If you know that a sale is pending, talk to the seller to try to make the buyer aware of them or talk to the buyer. If it is something of great importance and you can not contact the buyer directly, find out which escrow company they are using and send them a letter stating the agreement. If all else fails, get a lawyer.

FORECLOSURE

When property is purchased at a foreclosure sale, the leases of the tenants are terminated if they were signed after the date of the *Deed of Trust (mortgage)*. Any leases signed before the mortgage are still binding on the new owner.

RAISING THE RENT

If a *tenancy* is for a set term (such as a one-year lease) at a specified rent, then the landlord cannot raise the rent until the term ends, unless such right is spelled out in the lease. This is common in commercial leases where the term may be for several years. However, it is not prohibited in a residential lease.

Example: Your one-year lease could call for a rent increase after six months. There would have to be a set amount of the increase, like $100 or five percent, or a formula to determine the amount, like the increase in a consumer index.

This would be unusual. If you see something like this in a lease, be sure you understand it before you sign. Also, be sure it is not a way to avoid rent control laws. If the tenancy is month to month, then the landlord would be able to raise the rent by giving notice at least thirty days in advance. This is based upon the requirement of thirty days notice to terminate the tenancy and create a new one at the higher rent.

A **NOTICE OF CHANGE OF TERMS** is a typical form that a landlord would use to raise the rent in a month-to-month tenancy. (see form 16, p.171.) In such cases, you would not have to give thirty days notice if you decided not to stay until after the increase takes effect. This is because by raising the rent the landlord would be terminating the previous tenancy and making you an offer to enter into a new tenancy at a different rental rate.

THIRTY-DAY NOTICE

Most agreements call for the standard thirty-day notice since some courts have been reluctant to enforce the seven day increase. You should also be aware that any rent increase allows the landlord to increase your security deposit to the new maximum of two months rent for unfurnished and three months for a furnished unit. This is not always done.

California Civil Code, Section 1946, allows the parties to shorten the notice period when the rental agreement is created, to as little as seven days. Since terminating the agreement requires thirty days, raising the rent in seven days seems to give the landlord an unfair advantage. You can move if you do not want to pay the increase but can you do it in seven days?

SEVEN-DAY NOTICE

Even if you do have a seven-day notice requirement in your lease, the rent cannot be raised for any period when the rent has already been paid.

Example: If you paid your rent on June 1, for example, a seven-day notice given on June 2 would not be effective until July 1.

Certain cities have a different requirement for notice. Section 1946.1 sets out the requirement of 60 days for tenants occupying the property for more than one year, with several exceptions for Los Angeles, Santa Monica and West Hollywood. The tenant does not have to give 60 days notice to terminate the tenancy. Both Sections 1946 and 1946.1 are contained in Appendix A.

Most commonly, rent is increased on the date it is due (usually the first of the month). This is not a legal requirement, and rent may be raised on any date if the proper notice is given. If the rent is raised in the middle of a rental period, the landlord must prorate the rent. This means you pay the amount due before and after the increase on the next usual rent payment date.

Most rent increases are accomplished by mailing a notice to the tenant. Until January 1, 2001, this did not comply with the law (California Code of Civil Procedure, Section 1162) and worked only because the tenant did not object. The law required an attempt at *personal service* before mailing was acceptable. (I mention this because the new law expires in 2006 unless renewed.)

California Civil Code, Section 827 (the new law) allows mailing as an acceptable form of notice without first attempting to serve the tenant personally. Personal service is still allowed and Section 1162 is contained in Appendix A for your information. You will probably receive your notice by mail.

In 2006, the procedure changes and rent increases require thirty-days notice, but may be shortened by agreement to seven days (also designated as Civil Code Section 827, contained in Appendix A.)

Here is how it is *now* done by mail. The landlord may use the regular mail but must be able to prove that he sent it to the right address with proper postage. This can be done by affidavit. It is safer to do it by sending certified mail and usually done this way. Overnight mail and even a fax is acceptable if you have agreed to it in writing.

Here are the major changes in the 2006 law.

1. If the landlord uses the mail, he must allow extra time for the notice. If mailed in California—five extra days. If mailed outside of California but within the United States—ten extra days. If mailed outside the United States—twenty extra days.

2. If the landlord raises the rent more than 10% in a one-year period, he must give a 60-day notice. The 10% increase does not have to be all at once. For example, if the raise is 5% in January and 6% in July, the July increase will require a 60-day notice. The landlord is still required to add the extra time for mailing.

The relevant code section (California Civil Code, Section 827 until 2006) is contained at the end of the chapter. Procedural sections of the Code of Civil Procedure, Sections 1013 and 1162 are contained in Appendix A.

NOTE: *Rent control or any other government program, such as subsidized housing, may affect the landlord's ability to raise rents and security deposits, as well as affect the procedure for doing so.*

MODIFYING THE LEASE

If you agree to modify the terms of your lease, you should do so in writing. A simple modification form, AMENDMENT TO LEASE/RENTAL AGREEMENT is included in this book and will probably be similar to what the landlord will ask you to sign. If you are asked to sign something more complicated, be sure you understand it before signing. (See form 10, p.159.)

DAY CARE 7

If you operate or plan to operate a day care facility from your residence, you cannot be prevented from doing so. California Health and Safety Code Section 1597.40 allows this, even if your lease or rental agreement prohibits it *and* you are in violation of zoning laws.

LICENSE

However, there are some rules. You must have a license. The process of getting a license will include an inspection and certification of your residence. Once you have been approved and licensed, you must give the landlord a minimum of thirty days notice before starting to operate. If you already operate a day care facility and are moving, shorter notice may be given once your license is approved for your new residence.

SECURITY DEPOSIT

Your security deposit may be increased above that of other tenants, but it may not exceed the legal limit for security deposits.

OBLIGATION TO LANDLORD

Should you tell the landlord of your plans before moving in? I do not believe that you have an obligation to tell him. The law was passed to prevent landlords from discriminating against child care providers. If you tell the landlord of your plans before signing your lease or rental agreement and moving in, he may simply turn down your application. However, the law does not protect you in the operation of your business. If the children cause damage to the property, you will still be responsible.

Problems During the Tenancy 8

Even with good tenants, a good landlord, and a fair lease or rental agreement, there may still be problems. This chapter examines some of these problems from the legal prospective. It points out what the law allows and forbids the landlord from doing.

Landlord's Access to the Premises

California Civil Code, Section 1954 is specific about a landlord's right to enter a tenant's unit. According to the statute, the landlord has the right to enter a tenant's unit:

- in an emergency (the statute does not define emergency);

- to make necessary or agreed upon repairs, decorations, alterations, improvements, or services;

- to show the unit to prospective buyers, mortgagees, tenants, or workmen;

- when the unit has been abandoned or surrendered;

- pursuant to a court order; or,

- by invitation or consent of the tenant.

Except in cases of emergency, abandonment, or surrender, the landlord can enter only during normal business hours. The statute does not define normal business hours; however, lease forms that call for entry between 8 A.M. and 6 P.M., Monday through Saturday are common.

Except in cases of emergency, abandonment, or surrender, or when it is impractical, reasonable notice must be given. The statute defines reasonable notice as twenty-four-hour notice.

NOTE: *California Civil Code, Section 1953 prohibits a tenant's waiver of rights under Section 1954. This means that even if your lease or rental agreement gives the landlord the right to enter "anytime" or something similar, the landlord can only enter as described above.*

VIOLATIONS BY THE TENANT

BAD CHECK
The landlord's policy concerning payment by check and bounced checks should be set out in the rental agreement. Charges for bounced checks may also be posted where the rents are paid.

If you write a bad check, the rent is considered unpaid and you may be served with a THREE DAY NOTICE TO PAY RENT OR QUIT. (See form 21, p.181.) This means that you have three days to make the check good or face *eviction*. It also means that you have caused the landlord an unnecessary problem. You usually know if your check will clear. If there is a doubt, call and say that the check will be late rather than giving the landlord a bad one. Your word (reputation) is very important. When you give a check, you give your word that it is good.

Under California Civil Code, Section 1719, payment can be demanded by the landlord's sending by certified mail a letter that states the amount of the check and the amount of any charges. If your landlord makes this demand and the check is not made good within thirty days, he is entitled to three times the amount of the check, up to $1,500. The maximum that the landlord may charge for a bounced check is $25 for the first check and $35 for each check after that.

A NOTICE OF DISHONORED CHECK AND DEMAND FOR PAYMENT is included in this book in Appendix C. (See form 19, p.177.) If you stopped payment, the landlord must use a different procedure as explained in California Civil Code, Section 1719 in Appendix A.

If your rent check bounces, the landlord will probably give you a THREE DAY NOTICE TO PAY RENT OR QUIT and a thirty-day notice to make a check good. (See form 21, p.181.) He will do this so that he can possibly collect triple damages if you leave without making the check good. As you see, this can be a serious problem.

If the landlord holds the check, he can periodically call the bank to see if any money is in your account. A bank will usually cash a check less than six months old. If he re-deposits a bounced check and it bounces again, the bank will mutilate it (punch holes in it) and he will not be able to later cash it. This is important since months after you move the check could be cashed, causing you a shortage in your account and more bounced checks. If you are in this situation, start fresh by opening a new account.

Always try to keep the landlord informed that a rent payment will be late rather than giving him a post dated check or asking him to hold a check. Banks cash post dated checks without liability and there is nothing to prevent your landlord from depositing a check that he has promised to hold.

If you bounce a check because you are broke, it does not buy you much time and you are going to face eviction. Unfortunately, you might not be able to prevent being broke. However, bouncing a check because of poor timing is preventable.

If, for example, the check you will use to pay the rent comes on the seventh of the month, do not agree to a lease or rental agreement that calls for a late charge if rent is paid after the fifth. Do not count on the check that you give on the fifth not clearing until your check comes on the seventh. If the landlord is confident that a good check will be given on the seventh, eighth, or ninth, he will usually be willing to postpone late charges until then.

DAMAGE TO THE PROPERTY

Minor damage by a tenant, even if intentional, must be repaired by the landlord. The tenant may be billed for the cost involved. If the tenant does not pay, the landlord may sue for the amount due.

Major damage done by a tenant may relieve the landlord of the duty to keep the unit habitable. This is discussed further in Chapter 4. The landlord may bill the tenant for the damage, and sue if it is not paid.

The landlord may also serve the tenant with a THREE DAY NOTICE TO COMPLY OR QUIT, or obtain an injunction against the tenant doing further damage. (See form 22, p.183.) An attorney will usually be involved and costs will be high.

Example: You go away for the weekend and allow a friend to use your apartment. He throws a party and trashes the place. What to do?

If the party was that wild, your landlord is probably aware of it. Clean up as best you can. Write down the damage caused. Contact your landlord before he contacts you. Explain what happened and assure him that it will not happen again. Make some arrangement that will allow you a reasonable time to repair those things that you can. Then try to determine if you will be better off to hire someone to fix the rest or have your landlord take care of it. The most important thing is to get the landlord on your side as a victim of your friend, rather than someone who does not care about the property. A landlord usually can have things repaired at little cost, if he wants to do so.

If you violate the lease, for example, by making too much noise, having a pet or allowing too many people to live in the unit, the landlord has three options. If the breach is curable, he can send a THREE DAY NOTICE TO COMPLY OR QUIT. If the breach is incurable, he can give either a three or thirty-day notice to quit. (The procedure is explained in detail in Chapter 9, "Terminating a Tenancy.")

All of these problems can be easily solved by a good, common sense relationship with your landlord and with the other tenants. If you have an unreasonable landlord or unreasonable neighboring tenants, you can give in to their demands or stand your ground. If the landlord is the problem, first put your concerns in writing and then send them to him (always keep a copy). If you consider the problem more serious, have a lawyer write the letter. You may also consider a tenants' organization, as described in Chapter 16.

If other tenants are the problem, again put it in writing to the landlord. Battling directly with your neighbors is almost always a bad idea. If you have a bad landlord and bad neighbors and it is a really serious problem—either move, call a lawyer to break your lease, or sue for damages.

VIOLATIONS BY THE LANDLORD

The landlord may not retaliate against a tenant who has exercised any rights under California Civil Code, Section 1942. These rights include:

- a written or verbal complaint to the landlord;

- a complaint to any government agency;

- filing a lawsuit or arbitration proceeding; and,

- receiving a judgment or arbitration award.

Retaliation includes raising rent, decreasing services, and eviction. The burden is on the tenant to prove that the landlord is retaliating and not acting for some legitimate reason. The landlord's action must be within 180 days of the tenant's action in order to have a claim of retaliation.

The section then goes on to say that if a landlord's action to raise rent, decrease services or evict is disputed, the landlord must prove the legitimate purpose. As a practical matter, a landlord must have a provable reason that is not retaliatory in order to raise rent, reduce services, or evict. Penalties for violation may include punitive damages and attorney's fees.

BUILDING BECOMES UNINHABITABLE

Under California Civil Code, Section 789.3, a landlord who terminates or interrupts utilities such as water, heat, light, electricity, gas, elevator, garbage collection, or refrigeration can be held liable for up to $100 per day ($250 minimum) in damages, plus attorney's fees and actual damages suffered by the tenant.

Tenant duties. If the building becomes uninhabitable, the tenant has two duties and then three options. The two duties are:

- Notify the landlord. This may be done orally or in writing (writing is better).

- Give the landlord a reasonable time to make the repairs. A reasonable time will vary with the type of repair necessary.

More than thirty days is generally considered unreasonable for most repairs. The time may be much shorter for repairs such as no heat in the winter or broken water pipes.

Tenant options. If the landlord fails to repair in a reasonable time, the tenant may:

- Move, even if this would violate the terms of a lease or rental agreement;

- Repair and deduct. The tenant may make the necessary repairs and deduct an amount not to exceed one month's rent. This may be done not more than twice in a twelve month period (California Civil Code, Section 1942.); or,

● Withhold rent. This is a more complex remedy. Not only may the tenant refuse to pay rent until the defect is corrected, the tenant may demand reduced rent for the time that the property was not in proper condition.

The tenant must have the rent available, and cannot use this as a way to avoid paying rent. If a court decides to reduce the rent, or the landlord and tenant agree to a reduced rent, the tenant must pay it within three days if notice is given.

RECEIVERSHIP AND RELOCATION

In extreme cases, the California Health and Safety Code, Section 17980.7(c), allows for a *receiver* to be appointed to take over operation of the building, make necessary repairs, and pay for tenant's moving and relocation until the repairs are made.

NOTE: *Under California Health and Safety Code, Section 17980.7(b) 1 and 2, if the condition of the property violates state or local codes and the landlord does not make the necessary repairs within six months, the landlord may lose the tax advantages of the property, such as deductions for interest and depreciation allowed under California Revenue and Taxation Code, Sections 17274 and 24436.6. These are state rules and not federal.*

Sometimes pointing this out to a landlord (in writing) lets him or her know that you have some knowledge of the law and that you are a serious threat if he or she does not shape up.

DESTRUCTION OF THE PREMISES

If the premises are damaged by fire, earthquake, or other casualty, the rights of both landlord and tenant are usually spelled out in the lease. If the lease does not cover this situation, or if the rental is under an oral agreement, then California law provides that upon total destruction of the premises, the lease terminates. (California Civil Code, Section 1933.) If the premises are only partially destroyed, the tenant has the option of terminating the tenancy upon giving notice. (California Civil Code, Section 1932.)

It is a good excuse to break your lease or renegotiate it, but the damage has to have some effect on you. A dumpster fire is not going to be enough to let you break your lease. A fire in a unit close to you that requires substantial inconvenience to you during repairs may be enough. A fire in *your* unit that causes substantial damage is obviously enough.

Since this is a judgment call, discuss the matter with your landlord. If he disagrees, and you really believe that the law applies to your situation, get advice from a lawyer or a tenants' organization.

RESPONSIBILITY FOR MAINTENANCE   9

The duty of a landlord to maintain the property has increased over the years. Typically, the first thing most tenants do when something goes wrong is to call the landlord to fix it. This is true even if the tenant caused the problem. In most instances you will not have a problem with this unless there is a large amount of money involved. Landlords do not want minor repairs to become major repairs and know that many tenants may lack the money to make repairs immediately. Landlords usually have a "handyman" who makes minor repairs and is on salary so the cost to the landlord is small. Always determine in advance that the landlord is paying for the repairs. You do not want to get an unexpected bill after the repairs are completed.

If you are handy and are renting a house, you may make a deal with the landlord to do minor repairs and deduct the cost of materials from the rent. This not only saves the landlord money but gives you more privacy. There should be a maximum dollar amount set so there are no misunderstandings. Some landlords will allow tenants to make improvements as well as repairs. This benefits you by giving you a nicer place to live and increases the value of the property at a reduced cost to the landlord.

This usually works with a house rather than an apartment. If this idea appeals to you, discuss it with the landlord. Sometimes the landlord may want you to live in the house for six months or longer before allowing this. It does not hurt to ask.

LANDLORD'S DUTIES

Duties are created in two ways. You must do what you agree to do (this is your contractual duty) and you must also do what the law requires you to do. Let us look at both of these, starting with the contract (what you agree to do).

CONTRACT
BETWEEN
PARTIES

The contract between the parties, whether a written or verbal agreement, can impose an obligation on the landlord to provide certain types of maintenance beyond the legal requirements.

Example: If the lease allows use of a swimming pool or states that the landlord will paint the unit, then the landlord would be obligated under the agreement to maintain the pool and paint the unit.

However, since landlords typically provide the lease agreements, excessive promises are not usual and you should not expect them. Your protection will come from the legal obligations.

CALIFORNIA
CIVIL CODE

State law requires the landlord to keep the premises livable. The word used in the code is that a rental property cannot be "untenantable." California Civil Code, Section 1941.1, states that a property is untenantable unless it has:

(a)   effective waterproofing and weather protection of roof and exterior walls, including unbroken windows and doors;

(b)   plumbing or gas facilities that conform to applicable law in effect at the time of installation, maintained in good working order;

(c)   a water supply approved under applicable law, that is under control of the resident, capable of producing hot and cold running water, furnished to appropriate fixtures, and connected to a sewage disposal system approved under applicable law;

(d)   heating facilities that conformed with applicable law at the time of installation and are maintained in good worker order;

(e)   electrical lighting, with wiring and electrical equipment that conformed with applicable law at the time of installation, maintained in good working order;

(f)   building, grounds, and appurtenances at the time of the commencement of the lease or rental agreement in every part clean, sanitary, and free from all accumulations of debris, filth, rubbish, garbage, rodents, and vermin, and all areas under control of the owner kept in every part clean, sanitary, and free from all accumulations of debris, filth, rubbish, garbage, rodents, and vermin;

(g)   an adequate number of appropriate receptacles for garbage and rubbish, in clean condition and good repair at the time of the commencement of the lease or rental agreement, with the owner providing appropriate serviceable receptacles thereafter, and being responsible for the clean condition and good repair of such receptacles under his or her control;

(h)   floors, stairways, and railings maintained in good repair; and,

(i)   dead bolt locks on unit entrances are required by Civil Code Section 141.3 (see Appendix A.)

The common sense definition of being "untenable" is having serious defects that make it very difficult or impossible for the tenant to reside on the property. Cosmetic defects are not included. As explained above, the landlord may create a duty for cosmetic defects by agreement.

HEALTH CODES   Besides the habitability requirement of the statutes, there are various health codes both at the state and local level. Some of these are contained in the California Health and Safety Code, Section 17920.3, and Title 25 of the California Code of Regulations. Most local governments also have building and health regulations.

Most landlords are aware that governmental bodies can levy fines of hundreds of dollars a day for minor violations and ignoring notices of violation can be expensive. Getting government agencies involved is a powerful weapon if the landlord refuses to make repairs in a reasonable time that violate health and safety codes.

WAIVER OF LANDLORD'S DUTIES

As a basic rule, landlords cannot get out of their duty of maintenance by putting it on the tenant. (California Civil Code, Section 1942.1.) However, the statute contains an exception where the parties agree that the tenant shall do the maintenance in exchange for lower rent.

As a practical matter, only a small number of units would be suitable for tenant maintenance. The usual situation is the single family house. There must be a true agreement for reduced rent. If the court decides that the tenant has simply waived the right to the landlord's duty to repair and maintain the property, the agreement will not be enforced.

This is different from the informal agreement discussed above. This is a written agreement specifying the repairs to be made by the tenant and the amount of the reduced rent.

TENANT'S DUTIES

The duties of a tenant are set forth by California Civil Code, Section 1941.2, which provides:

(a)   No duty on the part of the owner to repair a dilapidation shall arise under Section 1941 or 1942 if the resident is in substantial violation of any of the following affirmative obligations, provided the resident's violation contributes substantially to the existence of the dilapidation or interferes substantially with the owner's obligation under Section 1941 or 1942 to effect the necessary repairs:

(1)   to keep that part of the premises which he occupies and uses clean and sanitary as the condition of the premises permits;

(2)   to dispose from his dwelling unit of all rubbish, garbage, and other waste in a clean and sanitary manner;

(3)   to properly use and operate all electrical, gas, and plumbing fixtures and keep them as clean and sanitary as their condition permits;

(4)   not to permit any person on the premises, who with his permission, willfully or wantonly destroys, defaces, damages, impairs, or removes any part of the structure or dwelling unit or the facilities, equipment, or appurtenances thereto, nor permits himself to do any such thing; and/or,

(5)   to occupy the premises as his abode, utilizing portions thereof for living, sleeping, cooking, or dining purposes only which were respectively designed or intended to be used for such occupancies;

(b)   Paragraphs (1) and (2) of subdivision (a) shall not apply if the owner has expressly agreed in writing to perform the act or acts mentioned therein.

The landlord may agree to perform the requirements of paragraphs (1) and (2). The agreement must be in writing.

If you keep the unit clean and do not destroy it or allow others to do so, you are okay. You cannot steal fixtures or appliances. You have to use plumbing, electricity, etc. as it was intended.

If you plan to run a business out of your unit, you may violate paragraph (5). I say "may" because no one is going to think much about it if your business is giving advice over the internet concerning motorcycle repair. If your business is repairing motorcycles in your living room, expect a problem. Common sense is the best guide.

Furnished Apartments

If you are renting a furnished unit, check your agreement for responsibility for broken furniture. Check all the furniture carefully to be sure it is in good condition. You are going to sign a paper that says that you checked it and found everything in good condition. You should list any defects on this form. If it is part of your lease or rental agreement, attach a sheet of paper listing the defects and have the landlord sign it.

Tenant's Remedies

If the landlord has failed to comply with his duty to do proper maintenance, the law offers you several possible remedies, depending on the severity of the situation.

If a landlord violates the maintenance requirements of the statutes or the health and safety codes and such violation renders the premises untenantable, then you can move out (break your lease) or withhold all or part of the rent until proper repairs are made.

Withholding Rent

Whether a tenant is legally entitled to withhold rent can only be determined in court, meaning the landlord would need to bring an action to either collect the rent or evict you. Since this is time-consuming, expensive, and risky, a smart landlord will usually work with you to correct the problems and have the rent paid voluntarily.

The claim that rent is being withheld for a maintenance violation is often made after the tenant has been taken to court for failure to pay rent. The law does not require the tenant to give the notice in writing or to produce proof of delivery, so a tenant can claim to have given notice after an eviction has been started. I do not advise lying to a judge but you may be advised by a lawyer or tenant group to do so. Follow your conscience.

RENTAL
DEDUCTION
FOR REPAIRS

If the problem with the premises renders the premises untenantable and the landlord fails to remedy it within a reasonable time, then the tenant is allowed to make the repair and deduct the cost from the next month's rent under California Civil Code, Section 1942. This remedy cannot be used more than twice in a twelve month period. Even though the code defines untenantable, as listed above, this is still a question of fact because the severity of the problem would have to be considered.

What is a reasonable time is also a legal question that depends on the facts. The law says that thirty days is clearly reasonable. But a much shorter time would also be reasonable for many problems.

The tenant must give the landlord reasonable notice of the problem before using this remedy. The notice can be verbal or in writing. The problem cannot be caused by the tenant or a violation of the tenant's duties.

If the premises are actually untenantable and the landlord refuses, after a reasonable amount of time, to remedy the situation, the tenant also has the option of moving out. A tenant using this remedy where there is substantial time remaining on the lease is taking a risk that he or she will be sued for breach of the lease. However, if you are trying to break your lease and genuinely get this situation, take advantage of it. You should get an opinion from a lawyer or tenants' group as to whether the premises are legally untenantable.

MOVING OUT

If the premises are actually untenantable, the landlord would be wasting time tracking you down and filing a suit. If the landlord believes that the problem is not serious and used as an excuse to break the lease, the landlord might want to take the matter to court. If so, you should be prepared with photographs and witnesses to prove that the condition of the premises was as bad as claimed.

TELEPHONES

The landlord is responsible for all wiring in the building for telephones, including being required to supply one telephone jack (California Civil Code Section 141.4).

The phone company currently charges $1.20 per month for a maintenance policy and $120 for a service call if you do not have the policy. There is no reason that you should pay for this.

OPTIONS   Pay for the policy yourself so you do not have to deal with the landlord if there is a problem.

A better option is to pay for the policy and deduct it from your rent. If you have a lease, you could deduct one year of payments from your twelfth month rental payment (about $15).

Forget the policy and simply call your landlord if there is a problem. If you live in a fairly new building, there will probably never be a problem.

When you are negotiating your lease, ask the landlord how he wants to handle it. There is no requirement that you buy the maintenance policy. If the landlord wants you to, he should reimburse you.

If you do not buy the policy, here is the procedure. When your phone does not work, first make sure that it is not in the lines outside your property. Plug another phone into the jack. If that phone does not work, ask a neighbor if her phone is working.

Once you have determined that it is just your phone wiring, use your neighbor's phone to contact the phone company. Your payment may have been lost or misplaced. They will also confirm that it is your wiring.

Once you have done all that, call the landlord to fix it.

HEALTH CONSIDERATIONS AND CALIFORNIA LAW 10

This is a separate chapter because I wish to call special attention to these subjects. They are important and the law is still evolving. When you read this, the law may be settled. If these subjects apply to your current situation, do further research or consult a lawyer.

MOLD

Recently, the health hazards of mold are being addressed by the legislature. Currently there is only legislation that creates a task force to formulate guidelines concerning the allowable amount of mold, cost considerations for eliminating it, and disclosure. Eventually, a booklet will be given to each tenant.

If you find mold in your unit, notify the landlord immediately. If the landlord ignores your problem or avoids fixing it, contact a lawyer. If you have expenses connected with the elimination of the mold, such as staying in a hotel, insist that the landlord pay them. If he refuses, sue in small claims court or contact a lawyer.

PROPOSITION 65

The Safe Drinking Water and Toxic Enforcement Act of 1986, commonly known as Proposition 65, requires a business (landlord) to post a warning of any dangerous chemicals that are on the property that pose a significant risk to you.

Since this requirement, lawsuits have been filed citing tobacco smoke and exhaust fumes from automobiles as toxic chemicals that landlords failed to properly warn against.

You will probably get a letter in addition to seeing posted signs stating that there is the danger that you will be exposed to tobacco smoke and vehicle exhaust fumes. You, of course, already know this and need not take any action based on the letter. However, if the landlord represented the property as a "smoke free" building or if cars are illegally parked on a regular basis very close to your apartment, you may wish to consult a lawyer.

If any other toxins are mentioned, be sure that you understand the possible danger. The law covers carcinogens (things that cause cancer) and reproductive toxins. If you are pregnant, ask your doctor about the effect of the chemicals. The law does not excuse the landlord from a negligence claim if dangerous chemicals could be removed and are not.

LANDLORD'S LIABILITIES 11

The law of liability for injuries and crime on rental property has changed considerably over the last couple of decades. The law for hundreds of years, that landlords are not liable, was overturned and landlords are now often liable, even for conditions that are not necessarily their fault. A great deal of this change was not made by legislators, but by judges who felt that tenants needed protection and that landlords should give it to them.

GENERAL RULES OF LANDLORD LIABILITY

The landlord has a duty to make safe conditions or adequately warn of dangerous conditions. However, warning is only a temporary safeguard until the premises can be made safe. This duty applies not only to what we usually think of as dangerous conditions, such as a broken step or cracked walkway, but to the actions of others. This means criminal acts by tenants and non-tenants may create liability for the landlord.

This can be very important to you. Say you are injured by another tenant. If you can hold the landlord responsible, you have a better chance of collecting compensation, since the tenant who injured you may not be able to pay.

In order to understand why someone is liable, let's examine the law.

There are three ways to create liability:

- intentional acts;

- negligence; and,

- strict liability.

INTENTIONAL ACTS

Example: A landlord assaults a tenant. Assault, by definition, is intentional. It is both a crime and what is called a *tort*. This means the landlord could be both prosecuted for the crime (fined or jailed) and sued by the tenant in civil court for damages (money).

NEGLIGENCE

If a landlord caused injury to a tenant through carelessness, it would not be intentional but would fall under the second category, *negligence*. The basis of the vast majority of liability is negligence. The chances of a landlord deliberately trying to injure you or damage your property are small compared to your being injured or your property damaged because the landlord was careless.

In order to have liability for negligence, four elements must be present:

Duty. The defendant (landlord) must owe a duty to the plaintiff (the one who is suing). Today that duty will extend to almost anyone who is injured on the property, not just a tenant. This would apply to visitors you may have.

Owing a duty to the plaintiff means that the relationship between the parties requires that the defendant must use reasonable care to avoid damage to the plaintiff.

Example: If a visitor to the building saw a discarded banana peel on the ground, the visitor would have no duty to remove it and would not be liable for any subsequent injury caused by slipping on it. The landlord, seeing the same peel, would have a duty to remove it, and would incur liability for a subsequent injury.

A duty may sometimes be created by the landlord where none previously existed.

Example: There may be no duty to have an alarm system in the building. However, if one is installed, the landlord may be liable if failing to keep it in good working order caused someone to be injured because it failed.

Breach of duty. A breach of duty is the failure to use reasonable care. This is usually what is contested. If the landlord did everything he reasonably could to prevent the damage or injury to the plaintiff, he is not liable.

This may be difficult to determine since "reasonableness" is subjective. A judge or jury may have a much different idea than the landlord's or your idea of what is reasonable.

The standard of care expected of the landlord is what determines reasonableness. For example, someone attempting to give first aid to an auto accident victim would be held to a higher standard if she were a doctor than someone without medical training.

The *standard of care* may be greater if the landlord makes promises beyond the normal standards. These promises commonly concern safety from crime and are contained in advertisements as well as direct communication with the tenant. The landlord may want to impress you by telling you how safe the building is and all the things that are done to keep it safe. This is fine if all that is said is true. If the landlord tells you that ten security guards with dogs patrol the building every night, it better be true. If there is only one security guard and you are mugged, the landlord can be liable.

This is another example of duty above what is required. There is no legal requirement to have ten security guards with dogs on patrol. However, if that is what is promised and that is what you are relying on, then that is what the landlord has to do.

Causation. The breach of duty by the landlord must have caused the plaintiff's injury or damages. If there was an inadequate lock on your door (failure to use reasonable care) but the burglar came in through the window, there was no causation.

Damages. The plaintiff must be injured or suffer some loss as a result of the negligent conduct of the landlord.

When you consider them, these are common sense rules. If the landlord does something he should not do or does not do something he should, and this causes injury or damage to you or your visitor, the landlord will be liable. If the landlord does not compensate you to your satisfaction, talk to a lawyer.

Another common basis for a landlord's liability is what is called *negligence per se*. This is a presumed or automatic failure to use reasonable care. It arises when a landlord violates a law. A common example would be failing to fence off a swimming pool, which is required by law. (You still need duty, causation, and damages.) This is like negligence, except there is no need to prove breach of duty.

STRICT
LIABILITY

The basis of strict liability is an unusually dangerous activity. If a landlord were having a fireworks display and something went wrong that caused injury, the fact that the landlord used reasonable care would not be a defense. The same would be true of injury caused by an animal normally considered a wild animal.

ACCIDENTS

The word accident can have two meanings. It can mean something that happens without fault by anyone. It can also mean something that could have, and should have, been prevented. The second meaning is the one creating liability.

A landlord is liable for failure to use reasonable care in keeping areas under the landlord's control safe for the tenants and others who may use them. This means that the landlord is liable if:

- the landlord created the dangerous condition;

- the dangerous condition would have been discovered by a reasonable inspection; or,

- the landlord knew of the dangerous condition.

The general rule is that a landlord is not liable for injuries on parts of the premises not under his control, except:

- where there is a danger known to the landlord;

- where there is a violation of law in the condition of the premises;

- where there is a preexisting defect in construction; or,

- where the landlord undertakes to repair the premises or is required by the lease to make the repairs.

PETS

The same rules that apply to accidents caused by dangerous conditions apply to injuries caused by pets. If the landlord knows that a pet owned by a tenant is dangerous, then the landlord can be liable if the pet injures someone.

How can a landlord know if a tenant's pet is dangerous? With most common types of cats and dogs the landlord will not know unless someone reports to the landlord that the pet is vicious.

However, if the pet is obviously dangerous (some consider all pit bulls to be dangerous), such as a poisonous snake (definitely both dangerous and illegal), then the landlord is assumed to know the condition is dangerous and would be liable for any injuries.

There is an old saying in the law that "every dog is allowed one bite." The theory is that you do not know that the dog bites until it bites someone. This is no longer true. Juries now award damages for the first bite. The difference is that they award more if they believe that the owner knew of the potential danger. If the landlord's dog bites you or your dog bites someone, there is going to be a settlement or a lawsuit. This is another reason to carry sufficient insurance.

When entering into your rental agreement or lease, look for a pet clause (See Chapter 5). It may give the landlord the right to evict you if your dog is determined to be dangerous. Also, be sure that your dog is approved for your tenant's insurance and the landlord's insurance.

CRIMES AGAINST TENANTS

Another area where liability of landlords has been greatly expanded is in the area of crimes against tenants. The current theory is that a landlord must protect tenants from crimes. Where the landlord can foresee the possibility of criminal attack, the landlord must take precautions to prevent it. But the law is still evolving in this area and some courts have interpreted this to mean that any time an attack is possible, the landlord must protect the tenant. This would include nearly every tenancy, especially in high crime areas.

INSTANCES WHEN A LANDLORD CAN BE LIABLE

RENTING TO A
DANGEROUS
TENANT

A landlord can be liable when he rents to a tenant who is dangerous where the landlord knows or should have known of the danger. Of course, it is difficult to know whether an applicant is dangerous. Using a person's looks to make such a determination could make the landlord liable for discrimination. If a tenant turns out to be dangerous after beginning a rental and the landlord fails to terminate the tenancy, the landlord could be liable for crimes committed by the tenant.

Most landlords do not run criminal background checks on prospective tenants, nor are they required to do so. However, an alert landlord or manager can spot signs of criminal activity, such as drug dealing or manufacturing. This must be dealt with as soon as discovered.

DANGEROUS
CONDITIONS

If windows do not lock properly, halls are not well lit, or bushes create good hiding places for muggers, this can create liability for the landlord.

INADEQUATE
SECURITY

In high crime areas, some courts have ruled that landlords can be liable for crimes if they fail to provide protection for their tenants and their guests in the form of security guards.

BROKEN
PROMISES

If a lease or advertisement for the property promises certain types of security, such as locked garages or security guards, then the landlord can be liable for failing to adequately provide them.

Problems at the End of the Tenancy 12

Most tenancies end without a problem. The tenant moves out as agreed and the security deposit is returned. There are, however, situations when it does not go this smoothly. This chapter examines these situations.

Holding Over

What happens if you do not leave at the end of your lease? If the landlord accepts rent after a lease expires, it creates a month-to month-tenancy. This is also called *holding over*.

At the end of a lease term, no notice is required by either landlord or tenant. However, since it is common for a tenant to stay after the end of the lease, you can expect one of the following:

- If the landlord does not want you to leave, he will accept rent. If he wants to raise the rent, he will serve a thirty-day notice before the lease term expires.

- If he wants you to leave, he will serve a THIRTY DAY NOTICE OF TERMINATION OF TENANCY, which will take effect at the end of the lease term. (See form 24, p.187.)

Unless you have had an awful relationship with your landlord, you should not have a problem. If you plan to stay, you will either sign a new lease or stay as a month-to-month tenant. You and your landlord will have discussed this in advance.

If you plan to leave, a problem arises if you do not leave on the scheduled date. This is only a real problem if the landlord has someone who is desperate to move in. This is why you get the TERMINATION OF TENANCY notice even though you have agreed to move out.

As a practical matter, there is not much that the landlord can do. The information in Chapter 15 shows how long it takes before you can actually be evicted. However, costs can be incurred. If you are having a problem because, for example, your new place is not ready, try to give the landlord a definite date when you will leave and ask that he not file suit before then.

DAMAGE TO THE PREMISES

If the landlord finds damage at the end of a tenancy, he may deduct the amount of the damage from your security deposit. This was discussed in Chapter 4, where the notice requirements were spelled out.

If the damages exceed the amount of the security deposit, the landlord may sue you. If they are under $5,000, the landlord can file the case in small claims court.

As was discussed in Chapter 4 before and after pictures as well as credible witnesses are a good way to avoid unjust charges. If you have caused damage to the property, try to get it fixed before leaving. This way you can have some control over the cost.

If you have made the landlord aware of the damage and he says that he will take care of it, try to get your security deposit back. If you have a $1000 security deposit, for example, and the landlord says he can get the damage fixed for $500 (and you are satisfied with that), try to get back the remaining $500 immediately. Then try to get the landlord to write (or at least say in front of witnesses) that the $500 he is keeping is your total liability. (This is not always possible, which is why I say "try.")

PROPERTY ABANDONED BY TENANT

Tenants often leave personal property behind when they move. It is usually of little value and in most cases the landlord throws it away. This is not, however, what the law requires.

If you leave property behind, the landlord must mail to you a Notice of Right to Reclaim Abandoned Property. You then have eighteen days from the date of the mailing to reply. The notice may be sent to the property if the landlord does not know where you are. If you filed a change of address with the post office, it will get to you.

If you do not reply to the notice, there are requirements based on the value of the property.

- If the property is worth less than $300, the landlord may do as he pleases with it.

- If the property is worth $300 or more, he must sell it at a public auction and the proceeds, less costs for storage, advertising and selling the property, must be turned over to the local county. You then have one year to claim the money.

There are specific requirements, including notice of the sale to the former tenant, advertising and hiring a bonded public auctioneer pursuant to Government Code, Section 6066, and Civil Code, Section 1988. Check these sections for the details if you want to know more about the procedure. They are contained in Appendix A.

As a practical matter, these auctions rarely occur. You are not going to leave personal property valued at $300 or more behind and never come back to claim it.

If you owe rent, the landlord may recover it from the proceeds of the auction only if he has a judgment against you, in which case he must properly levy against the proceeds of the auction.

If you contact the landlord for the return of the property, he may not refuse to return it until unpaid rent is paid. He may insist on reasonable storage charges. If a landlord refuses to return your property (valued at over $300) for any reason and proper procedures have not been followed for an auction, consult an attorney.

MOTOR
VEHICLES

If you leave a motor vehicle on the property, the landlord can sometimes get the police to tow it away and take responsibility for its disposal. However, some cities have different procedures and the landlord may have to arrange for towing, usually with a towing company. Most likely they will tow it, sell it, and deduct their fees from the proceeds. If there are excess proceeds, the landlord may be able to levy on them for any back rent judgment. If the vehicle has any value to you, get it (tow it if it will not run) to a safe place. Once a towing company starts running up the charges, you will never get it back.

TERMINATING A TENANCY 13

There are different types of tenancies, such as those involving a lease and those with a rental agreement. There are also special rules for public housing. In addition, either the landlord or the tenant can terminate. This chapter examines how to terminate and points out ways that are not allowed.

TENANCIES WITH NO SPECIFIC TERM

When there is no specific term, either party may terminate by giving written notice based on the rental period. A month-to-month tenancy requires at least a thirty-day notice. A week-to-week tenancy requires at least a seven-day notice. (California Civil Code, Section 1946).

The parties may agree to as short as a seven-day notice for a month-to-month tenancy. It is a bad idea to agree to a seven-day notice. If you do agree to one, be aware that the seven days cannot terminate the tenancy during a period for which the rent is already paid.

The law does not require termination to coincide with the payment of rent. If you pay rent on the first of each month and give a thirty-day notice on the tenth, you may legally vacate thirty days later without liability for rent after that date. The rent is due and payable up to and including the date of termination.

You do not have to give a reason to terminate a tenancy unless you have a lease that has not yet expired. You then need a "legal excuse," as discussed below. In most cases this is also true of the landlord. However, he cannot terminate a tenancy for an illegal reason, such as retaliation or discrimination. In public housing and some rent controlled areas he must always have a legally acceptable reason.

To terminate a month-to-month tenancy the landlord will use a THIRTY-DAY NOTICE OF TERMINATION OF TENANCY. A copy is provided to familiarize you with the document. (See form 24, p.187.) For a weekly rental, or a rental where you have agreed in writing to seven days notice, the landlord can change the "30" to "7" on the notice.

The notice can be personally handed to you anywhere or to another person at the property with a copy mailed to you. The notice can also be posted on the front door of the property and a copy mailed to you. If the landlord sends the notice by certified or registered mail, add five additional days to the time to terminate.

NOTE: *If you are under rent control or have Section 8 housing, always check the requirements. Your notice requirement can be as much as ninety days.*

EXPIRATION OF RENTAL OR LEASE TERM

When the term of a lease ends, you are expected to vacate the property without notice. This is different from some states where you may have lived that presume a lease is renewed unless the tenant gives the landlord notice that she is leaving.

Even if you plan to move and your landlord knows this, you may be served with a THIRTY-DAY NOTICE thirty days before your lease expires. Landlords do this as a precaution. You may also receive a LETTER TO VACATING TENANT, also nothing to worry about. (see form 17, p.173.)

What happens if you do not move? If the landlord accepts rent after the lease terminates, it is presumed to convert to a periodic (month-to-month) tenancy. This is fairly common and may be agreeable to all concerned. However, if the landlord wants you out, he will have to evict you. Eviction is covered in detail in Chapter 15.

Special requirements for termination apply to public housing. For more information, see the section on "Special Rules for Public Housing" on page 14.

EARLY TERMINATION BY TENANT

There are several reasons for you to terminate the tenancy early. Some of them are legally justified and some not.

UNINHABITABLE PREMISES

As discussed earlier, if the premises are destroyed, such as by fire or earthquake, you may immediately vacate the premises and terminate the rental. (California Civil Code, Section 1933.) If the premises are damaged so that the premises become uninhabitable, as defined in California Civil Code, Section 1941.1, and the landlord has not improved (or cannot improve) the conditions within a reasonable time, you may vacate the premises and terminate the rental.

BREACH OF AGREEMENT

If you leave the premises before the end of the lease agreement, and without the legal right to do so, you have breached the agreement (contract). The landlord then has two options:

- The landlord may re-rent the property and sue you for the unpaid rent during the time the property was vacant. The landlord's duty to mitigate is met if reasonable efforts are used to find another tenant.

  To mitigate damages means to make them as small as reasonably possible. I personally know of situations where the tenant moved out before the lease expired. People were lined up to rent the unit and move in the day the tenant moved out (at a higher rent). They not only did not have to pay damages for breach of the lease but got all their security deposit back.

You may not be so lucky. If the unit is difficult to rent, the unpaid rent is your responsibility until a new tenant is finally found or your lease expires. Ask the landlord what he intends to do to fill the vacancy and make sure he does it.

You should make every effort to find someone to take your place. If you present a qualified prospective tenant to the landlord, he must either accept the tenant or he has failed to mitigate. The tenant must be "acceptable." Someone with sufficient legal income and reasonably good credit would qualify.

● The landlord's other option is to ignore the duty to mitigate and hold you liable for the unpaid rent until the lease expires. California Civil Code, Section 1951.4 allows this only if the lease contained a notice of the landlord's intent to do this, and the lease:

- allowed subletting or assignment;

- allowed subletting or assignment with reasonable standards or conditions; or,

- allowed subletting or assignment with the landlord's consent, which will not unreasonably be withheld.

This clause does you no good. If you are allowed to assign or sublet, it will always be with the landlord's reasonable consent. This means that you have to find an "acceptable tenant," as stated earlier. Only now the burden is on you alone. The landlord has no obligation to find another tenant (mitigate). If you see such a clause, object to it before you sign your lease. A court may decide that the landlord has not done enough to mitigate even when the landlord thinks that he has. Do not relieve him of this duty if you can help it.

ABANDONMENT

Example 1: You have lost your job. You are going to have to move back to Ohio. You cannot pay the rent and still have enough money for gas. You move out in the middle of the night. What is going to happen? Probably nothing. The landlord will rent your unit and do nothing more. What could happen? The landlord could get a judgment against you for the unpaid rent and the judgment could be enforced in Ohio.

Example 2: You quit your job and take an extended vacation before starting your new (better) job. You give all your furniture and clothes to your brother-in-law because you are going to buy all new stuff. You return from your vacation five weeks later and discover that your unit has been rented to someone else and your refrigerator was confiscated by the landlord.

Check your mail. If you find no notices from the landlord, contact a lawyer. The landlord *must* take proper procedural steps before renting your unit to a new tenant. Many landlords do not take these steps because of the time and expense involved. Even if you find a Notice of Abandonment or a Three-day Notice for Nonpayment of Rent, check with a lawyer to make sure they were correctly served and are the proper forms. Cases where a landlord has improperly rented a unit believed to be abandoned have been settled for thousands of dollars. You could find a lawyer willing to work on contingency or very little up front costs, especially if the violation is clear and the case can be settled out of court.

Early Termination by Landlord

A landlord may terminate a tenancy before the end of the term for three reasons:

- failure to pay rent;

- failure to cure a curable breach of a covenant or condition of the lease; and,

- committing an incurable breach of a covenant or condition.

Failure to Pay Rent

Failure to pay rent is the most common reason for eviction. The landlord serves a THREE DAY NOTICE TO PAY RENT OR QUIT. (See form 21, p.181.) The notice may be served any time after the rent is due. The unlawful detainer action may be brought on the fourth day after the notice is served.

There is no grace period for rent payment unless the lease states so. However, allowing a tenant to continually pay rent late may modify your agreement or waive the landlord's right to rent on the agreed upon date. If you consistently pay your rent late, keep a record of the dates and your canceled checks. You could argue to a court that the three-day notice was improper. This could get you some valuable time when you need it most. Many landlords routinely serve a three-day notice any time the rent is late. This preserves their right to insist on rent as agreed to in the lease or rental agreement.

A THREE-DAY NOTICE TO PAY RENT OR QUIT must be completed and served exactly as required by law or the landlord can lose his eviction suit. The most important requirements follow.

CALCULATING THE THREE DAYS

This may sound simple, but many landlords have lost their case by making an error here. First, he must not serve the notice until the day after the rent is due. Even if you tell the landlord that you cannot pay the rent on the day it is due, he must wait until the next day to serve the notice.

Next, if the due date was a Saturday, Sunday, or legal holiday, he cannot serve the notice until the day after the next business day. Third, you do not count the day of service of the notice in the three days. Fourth, if the third day of the three day notice is a Saturday, Sunday or legal holiday, he cannot file for eviction until the day after the next business day.

Example: Suppose rent is due on the 25th of the month, and December 25th falls on a Friday. Since that day is a holiday, rent would not be due until Monday the 28th. The landlord would not be able to serve proper notice until the 29th, and since the 1st of January is a holiday followed by a weekend, the third day would be the 4th of January. Therefore, he could not file suit until the 5th. You can see that you should not assume that the notice was served at the proper time.

CALCULATING THE AMOUNT DUE

On a **Three Day Notice to Pay Rent or Quit** the landlord can only demand rent that is actually past due, not late fees or any other amounts due under the rental agreement.

NOTE: *If you are under rent control or have Section 8 housing, always check the requirements. Your notice requirements may differ.*

Curable Breach

A *curable*, but uncured, *breach of a covenant* or *condition* is a situation when the landlord wants you to stop doing something that violates the lease. Examples would include getting a pet or having a guest stay longer than permitted. **A Three Day Notice to Comply or Quit** is served. The form is provided so that you are familiar with it when it is served to you. (see form 22, p.183.)

If the problem is not corrected, the unlawful detainer action may be filed on the fourth day after the notice is served. Calculate the three days as described above to make sure it is served properly.

INCURABLE BREACH

An *incurable breach of a covenant* or *condition* is a situation when the landlord feels that you have done something so bad that he simply wants you out. Unauthorized assignment, severe damage to the property or assault of another tenant would be examples. If this type of situation exists, you will get a THREE DAY NOTICE TO QUIT. (see form 23, p.185.) An attorney will probably be involved since this is a more complex procedure. Your best defense is to convince a court that your action is curable and the landlord should have sent the THREE DAY NOTICE TO COMPLY OR QUIT. (see form 22, p.183.) You will know if you did something so bad that it cannot be rectified.

Knowingly allowing a drug-dealing tenant to remain in possession may subject a landlord to liability for damage or injury to other tenants, tenant's guests, workers, neighbors, and anyone else who could foreseeably be damaged or injured. In extreme cases, forfeiture of the property could result. If you are a victim of such a tenant, contact a lawyer. It is much safer to sue a landlord than a drug dealer.

Suppose you are accused of being the drug dealer. To accuse someone of dealing drugs could subject the landlord to liability. If you are wrongfully accused and given a three-day notice, contact a lawyer. Remember, we are not talking about *using* drugs. It is *dealing* that requires the landlord to act.

If you have a fixed term lease or are in a rent control property, it will be even more difficult for the landlord to evict you, as long as your rent is paid.

SPECIAL RULES FOR PUBLIC HOUSING

For non-payment of rent for a public housing unit the landlord must give the tenant a fourteen-day notice rather than a three-day notice. It must be mailed or hand delivered, not posted. (Code of Federal Regulations, Title 24, Section 866.4(1)(2).) The notice must inform the tenant of her right to a grievance procedure. Even an inability to pay the rent has been accepted as a valid reason for nonpayment.

SECTION 236
APARTMENTS

For breach of the terms of the lease other than payment of rent, a thirty-day notice must be given, except in emergencies, and it must inform the tenant of the reasons for termination, her right to reply, and her right to a grievance procedure. (Code of Federal Regulations, Title 24, Section 366(4)(1).)

For non-payment of rent, tenants must be given the three-day notice and be advised that if there is a judicial proceeding, they can present a valid defense, if they have one. Service must be by first class mail and hand delivered or placed under the door. (Code of Federal Regulations, Title 24, Section 450.4(a).)

For breach of the terms of the lease other than payment of rent, the tenant must first have been given notice that in the future such conduct would be grounds for terminating the lease. The notice of termination must state when the tenancy will be terminated, specifically why it is being terminated, and it must advise the tenant of the right to present a defense in the eviction suit. (Code of Federal Regulations, Title 24, Section 450.)

SECTION 8
HOUSING

Under the Code of Federal Regulations, Title 24, Section 882.215(c)(4), the landlord must notify the housing authority in writing at the commencement of the eviction proceedings. Also, the previous paragraph applies to Section 8 housing as well.

DEATH OF A TENANT

If a lease contains a clause binding the "heirs, successors, and assigns" of the lessee, then the lease continues after the death of the tenant unless cancelled by the lessor and the heirs. Otherwise, it is a personal contract that expires at the tenant's death because of impossibility of performance. If your lease contains the "heirs, successors and assigns" language, your estate will be liable for the rent. This could be a problem, especially if you live alone and have children. You have no one to take over your lease and the children could get less of your estate. Try to negotiate a personal lease contract. As a practical matter, the landlord will probably want to re-rent the property as soon as possible.

There is also the question of your personal property. If you are very ill or otherwise concerned about impending death, give the landlord written permission to turn your things over to a specific person. This could save storage charges to your estate. The landlord will probably follow your request, although he does not have to.

OPTIONS TO CANCEL

Some landlords like to use a lease form giving them an option to cancel the lease. However, when a lease allows one party to cancel it at will, the lease is not considered binding and the courts will allow either party to cancel it at will. A lease will probably be held to be valid if the option to cancel is contingent upon some event.

Example: A lease that gave the landlord the option to cancel if the property were condemned for a freeway would probably be valid.

If your lease contains an option to cancel for no specific reason, consider it a month-to-month agreement. If you want a longer term, object to the clause. The landlord may have a specific reason for the clause that is acceptable to you. If so, put that in as the *contingency* rather than the *at will* cancellation.

Reasons For Eviction 14

This chapter explains the basic steps of the eviction process.

There are three basic reasons for eviction:

- violating the terms of your lease or rental agreement. The most common violation is the failure to pay rent. Other reasons might be having a pet or subletting if prohibited by the lease;

- staying after your lease has ended; or,

- legal violations. This means violating the law (selling drugs, assaulting the landlord) rather than specific violations of your lease or rental agreement.

Violating Terms of the Rental Agreement

LATE RENT Let us start with the most common. You are late with your rent, which is a violation of your rental agreement.

Unless you have a grace period in your lease, you must pay your rent on the day it is due. By law rent is due at the end of the rental period unless otherwise agreed. Your rent will be due at the beginning of the rental period. This is almost always on the first of the month. If you have a grace period, you must pay by the last day of that period. The next day the landlord has the right to start the eviction process.

Let us say you are late because you are temporarily short of money or you had an unexpected expense or a check you normally receive is delayed. In other words you can pay the rent, just not on time.

Talk to the landlord or management company and explain the situation. Give a definite date when you can pay. They may still serve the three-day notice but rarely will they proceed to a court action if the delay is only a week or two. You can also offer, if you are able, to make a partial payment until you can pay in full. The most important thing is the definite date that you will pay. If you do not have one, the landlord will probably not agree to any delay.

UNABLE TO PAY RENT

You do not have the money and it is not coming in any time soon. For example, you have lost your job. Now you have two possible problems. You have a place to move to (friend or relative) but no money to move, or you have no place to move and are just stalling for time until you can come up with a place.

If it is simply a question of a few hundred dollars to rent a truck to move furniture and appliances, again talk to the landlord. Offer to move out immediately (no longer than one week) in exchange for moving money. It might sound like you are pushing it to ask someone that you owe money to and probably will never repay to give you more money. It is not. If you simply did nothing until you got evicted, it would cost the landlord more in lost rent and court fees than giving you your moving money. If you fight the eviction, it will cost him even more. Much more.

Landlords know this and are usually willing to pay to get the property back. They are also afraid that you will cause damage to the property in retaliation for their refusal. This, of course, is not advised, nor is the threat to do so. I mention it only so you know what the landlord may be thinking.

If you can not get enough money to move or have no place to go, I suggest that you contact a tenants' rights group in your area. They will have local information for emergency assistance. They may also suggest delaying tactics, including bankruptcy, to stall the eviction. Bankruptcy temporarily stops all proceedings but will reflect on your credit as well as causing possible loss of assets. Let your conscience be your guide in deciding on which tactics to use.

DO NOT PAY RENT IN PROTEST

A more complicated situation is that you are deliberately late with your rent to protest something the landlord has done or failed to do.

This could be due to a failure to repair something necessary for habitability, such as a broken heater in winter or a severe plumbing problem. It could also be that you finally had the repair done and are deducting the amount it cost you from your rent.

You also could be reacting to a discrimination issue. The landlord has raised your rent by a substantial amount while other tenants got no increase or a much smaller increase. Your rent is now substantially higher than other tenants with similar units. You believe that this was done to encourage you to move because of your race or because you reported the landlord to the building inspector for code violations (retaliation). You, of course, want to fight back.

CORRECTING YOUR VIOLATION

If you *are* violating a term of your rental agreement or lease, you might receive a type of three-day notice that requires you to do or stop doing the thing which violates your agreement. This is the **THREE-DAY NOTICE TO COMPLY OR QUIT**. It could be that you got a dog or moved in some friends in violation of your lease. Again, you may want to fight this. If you lost your sight, for example, and now need a dog to help you, the landlord cannot stop you from getting one. Maybe the friend staying with you is a guest who has not been in the property as long as the landlord believes.

STAYING AFTER YOUR LEASE TERM ENDS

When your lease is over, the landlord can refuse to accept any more rent from you and file an action for *Unlawful Detainer* (eviction) if you do not voluntarily leave. If the landlord accepts rent, however, the tenancy becomes a month-to-month rental.

Even though your lease is over, the same prohibitions against discrimination and retaliation apply and you may contest the eviction.

LEGAL VIOLATIONS

Your landlord might try to evict you if he or she thinks you are involved in a violation of the law. For example, your landlord might wrongfully accuse you of selling drugs. These situations almost always require a lawyer. Consult a lawyer for a possible defamation suit as well as for fighting the eviction.

With violations of law there may be police involved as well as the landlord, which is another reason to consider consulting an lawyer.

Dealing with Eviction 15

Lawyers

When dealing with your landlord and the possibility of eviction, you may want to consult an attorney if you feel that you are being asked to agree to something that could cause you trouble. As with any professional, you want a good one. How can you find one?

While lawyers are presumed to be competent to practice most area of the law, some lawyers are much, much better at a certain area of the law than others. The way I suggest to find a lawyer is to call your local bar association and ask for a state certified specialist near you. This is a lawyer who has many hours of experience in your problem area and has passed a test on the subject. They will give you several names. Make appointments and find one you like. Usually, there is either no charge or only a nominal charge for the first visit.

The state certified specialist will often charge more per hour than one who is not certified. However, you will almost always pay less in the long run. The specialist will usually do the work in a fraction of the time it would take another lawyer. Most importantly, you will have confidence in the advice you get.

Suppose that in spite of all your efforts, you have problems with your attorney. You believe that the fee charged for what you got is unfair. What do you do?

The California Bar Association requires arbitration of an attorney's fee when the client requests it. Call your local bar association or the Office of Mandatory Fee Arbitration at 415-538-2020, or type "California State Bar" into any Internet search engine.

If you want to go forward on your own, the same court proceedings for eviction apply.

Before Eviction

THIRTY-DAY
NOTICE OF
TERMINATION

When your landlord intends to evict you, he or she may first serve you with a THIRTY-DAY NOTICE OF TERMINATION OF TENANCY. (see form 24, p.187.) The landlord may serve this notice without giving a reason why he wants you out. Does this mean that there is nothing you can do? Not necessarily. If the landlord's (unstated) reason is discrimination or retaliation, for example, you can successfully fight the eviction.

If you are in a city with rent control, are under some type of government subsidized or public housing or are in the military, always check with the appropriate authority. The landlord's requirements and ability to evict you may differ greatly from rental units not under government control.

The only ways a landlord may recover possession of what the law calls a "dwelling unit" are:

- if you voluntarily surrender it to the landlord;

- if you abandon it; or,

- if the landlord gets a court order giving him possession.

SELF-HELP BY LANDLORD
Under California Civil Code, Section 789.3, landlords are specifically forbidden to use *self-help methods* to evict tenants, such as interrupting utilities, changing locks, removing doors or windows, or removing the tenant's personal belongings from the unit. Violation subjects the landlord to liability for a penalty of up to $100 per day, plus attorney's fees and any actual damages suffered by the tenant.

BEGINNING THE EVICTION PROCESS

The following is based on the landlord filing the suit, which is the most common situation. Various forms are used in this process.

Each county in the state of California makes its own rules regarding forms. Some have their own required forms. Some have optional forms. Some do not have forms. We have included forms in this book that should work in most areas. There are both forms that the landlord uses so that you can become familiar with them and the forms you will use. Before using them, you should ask your court clerk if they have any required or recommended forms.

COMPLAINT
An eviction is started by filing a complaint. An *eviction suit* is called an *unlawful detainer action*. The complaint must be filed in a division of Superior Court and a filing fee must be paid.

A COMPLAINT—UNLAWFUL DETAINER is included in this book as form 27 in Appendix C. You should go over it carefully to familiarize yourself with the form and what to look for if you get one.

Once the case is filed, you should not pay rent unless you can do so without signing a stipulation or are advised by an attorney to do so. If you pay rent without a stipulation that it will not affect the case, the case can be dismissed and the landlord will have to start over again with a new NOTICE and COMPLAINT. Try to get advice from a lawyer or tenants' organization for your particular situation.

SUMMONS   The SUMMONS is notice to you that you are being sued. (See form 28, p.197.) It should include the names of all adults living in the premises. If there are people living there whose names the landlord does not know, you will see them listed as John Doe, Jane Doe, etc.

If there are any adults living with you that the landlord does not know, he should serve a PREJUDGMENT CLAIM OF RIGHT TO POSSESSION. (See form 29, p.199.) with the SUMMONS (form 28) and COMPLAINT (form 27). This provides legal notice to everyone at the premises. Any unnamed occupant then has ten days to file the PREJUDGMENT CLAIM OF RIGHT TO POSSESSION. If this is not done, the claim cannot be made when the marshal or sheriff comes to actually evict the tenant. If it is done, the claimant will then be added to the action. If the landlord does not serve this form and someone he has not served claims to have a right to live there, it will delay the eviction.

Although anyone 18 or over who is not a party to the suit may serve the summons or complaint; the prejudgment claim can only be served by a sheriff, a marshal, or private process server.

NOTE: *If a friend or relative of the landlord serves the papers, check even more closely for errors. A landlord too cheap to use professionals is probably doing the work himself, without legal advice.*

In Section 8 housing, the local housing authority must be notified in writing before the tenant can be served with the eviction. (Code of Federal Regulations, Title 24, Section 882.215(c)(4).)

The papers served are a copy of the COMPLAINT with a copy of the SUMMONS stapled on top. After service is made, the person performing the service must return the original summonses to the court.

After the COMPLAINT and SUMMONS have been served, you have five days (excluding the day they are served and any legal holidays) to file an answer. At this point most tenants move out and the landlord can request that a default judgment be entered on the sixth day (unless it falls on a Saturday or Sunday, then it would be entered on Monday). However, if you file any type of answer with the court, there is no default.

ANSWER | Your ANSWER—UNLAWFUL DETAINER is straight forward. (See form 30, p.201.) You check a series of boxes that describe your position. You answer that either all or some of the landlord's claims in the complaint are false. You then briefly explain why you believe they are false.

If the landlord's claims are true, you then go to the boxes under number 3. These boxes are for what are called "Affirmative Defenses." You check the box or boxes that apply and briefly explain each on the second page.

Remember, be brief. You are not now trying your case. If there is a payment, for example, that is disputed, you can simply state that the payment was made. You do not need canceled checks or witnesses at this time.

NOTE: *Special rules apply to military personnel. There will not be a default judgment entered unless the tenant has an attorney. The landlord will usually contact the tenant's commanding officer before beginning eviction.*

PREPARING FOR TRIAL

NEGOTIATION | This is an excellent time to negotiate with the landlord. He will most likely, if he has not already, consult a lawyer to determine the cost to evict you. If there is something you want in return for moving, it will probably be cheaper (and certainly less time consuming) for him to give it to you. If you are able to talk to the landlord, tell him that you are going to demand a jury trial. His costs now increase again.

Do not misunderstand. If you simply can not pay the rent because you do not have the money and have no claim against the landlord, the court will not let you get any further than a hearing. You *must* have some reason to go to trial. If you do have a claim that can be settled by paying you to move or making changes and allowing you to stay, your negotiating position is strong at this time. Once the landlord has hired (paid) a lawyer to fight you, he may as well proceed.

The courthouse, just before a hearing, is a good place and time to negotiate. Even a landlord with a good case is nervous. Since there is no way of knowing how a trial will turn out, and even the best cases have been lost over a small mistake, most lawyers prefer to settle a case whenever possible. If you are able to settle with the landlord, you have an option. You can enter into a *stipulation to delay* the case or a *stipulation for entry of judgment* in the case. A stipulation is a contract entered into a court record.

If it will take time to work out the details of the agreement, you will delay the case. However, if you settle everything on the spot, you will go directly to JUDGMENT. (see form 32, p.211.) A judgment will be issued that reflects the agreement with your landlord. A typical stipulation might allow you to stay for a longer time than if eviction procedures were followed and call for some periodic payments of past-due rent. If the arrangement you have worked out does not fit the judgment form provided in this book, you can retype it to conform to your agreement.

If you are able to negotiate, be specific. If it is money you want, set the amount so that it is cheaper to pay you than fight you. If you withheld rent because you wanted some change made, estimate the cost of the change and the strength of your case. You can get help with this from a lawyer or a tenants' organization.

Preparing and going to trial will mean time off from work and much aggravation. Do not let emotions cause you to begin something you will regret. Having said that, if you have a good case and believe in what you are doing, you can proceed and win, possibly much more than what it costs you.

DISCOVERY   A request for discovery is another step in the trial preparation process. *Discovery* is a process by which parties can ask each other questions (either written ones called *interrogatories* or oral ones called a *deposition*) under oath. They can also subpoena each other's records, including bank statements and charge card receipts. Failure to respond can result in being held in contempt of court and giving false information can result in a criminal charge of perjury.

Discovery is a powerful tool in your lawsuit if the landlord is making claims that he cannot back up.

Example: If the landlord has estimates to repair damage you caused, the actual estimates may show that they came from a relative or were printed up by the landlord himself.

A sample discovery questionnaire called FORM INTERROGATORIES—UNLAWFUL DETAINER is provided in Appendix C. (see form 31, p.203.) You can also request a deposition where verbal questions are asked and recorded.

If you get to a deposition, you are well beyond the scope of this book. There are books devoted entirely to the trial process. They are the next best thing to hiring an attorney.

SETTING A
TRIAL DATE

The next step will be setting a trial date. This is done by filing either a Memorandum to Set Civil Case for Trial or a Request for Trial Setting, depending on the county you are in. This form can be obtained from the court clerk. The trial date will be set and a trial will follow in approximately two or three weeks.

TENANT
DEFENSES

If you have a hearing or trial, you will probably present one or more of the following defenses. The particular defenses may depend on the reason for eviction. Common defenses include:

- If you are being evicted for nonpayment of rent, you may argue that the landlord failed to keep the building habitable, which excuses the nonpayment of rent. If you notified the landlord of repairs that he failed to make before he served the three-day notice, this could be a persuasive argument. Even better would be if the landlord had been cited by a government inspector for health or safety violations.

- If you are not being evicted for nonpayment of rent, the more common arguments are retaliation, discrimination, or violation of a rent control ordinance. These, as well as habitability, have been covered earlier.

- You may also argue that the landlord did not follow proper legal procedure in serving your Notice or Summons and Complaint. Failing to properly fill out the forms may result in his having to start over. If this is what happens, you are in a great bargaining position. Be ready for the landlord to approach you.

WINNING YOUR CASE

To win your case you will need to prove that the claims in the landlord's complaint are either untrue or that you have a valid defense and/or counterclaim.

Here are three simple examples:

Example 1: The landlord says that you did not pay your rent. You deny this and show canceled checks showing payment in full.

Example 2: The landlord says that you did not pay your rent. You admit this but say that you withheld the rent because the property is uninhabitable (a legally acceptable reason).

Example 3: The landlord says that you did not pay your rent. You admit this but say that you withheld the rent because the landlord refused to make necessary repairs. You had the repairs done and paid more than the rent owed. The landlord actually owes *you* money (counterclaim).

TRIAL

The trial is usually held in the following manner, but ask your judge before you start because he or she may prefer a less formal procedure.

- opening remarks by the judge;

- landlord's opening statement;

- tenant's opening statement;

- landlord's testimony and evidence;

- tenant's testimony and evidence;

- landlord's rebuttal and closing argument;

- tenant's closing argument; and,

- landlord's rebuttal to tenant's closing argument.

OPENING
STATEMENT

In your opening statement, tell the judge what the case is about and what you plan to prove. Say which of the landlord's claims are untrue and those for which you have a legally acceptable defense. You should not present evidence at this time. You can say things like "I will present witnesses to prove that … or I will present documents to prove that…," but leave it at that.

TESTIMONY

In your testimony and evidence you go point by point through the complaint, disputing each one for one reason or another. Present evidence to back your argument whenever it is available.

CLOSING

In your rebuttal and closing argument you point out what parts of the landlord's evidence are untrue (if any) and argue that even if some points are true, you should win the case anyway because you have a legally acceptable defense.

JUDGE'S
DECISION

Once both sides have finished their presentation, the judge may announce a decision or say that the case will be taken under advisement. The reason for the latter may be that the judge wants to research the law, or perhaps thinks the parties are too emotional and might get upset. If a decision is made on the spot, you will obviously know your situation. If it is taken under advisement, you will receive the judgment in the mail within a few days.

OUTCOME OF
TRIAL

If you win, you will get whatever relief you sought. If you lose the case, your landlord will bring a prepared Writ of Execution to the court clerk. The Writ of Execution is then taken to the office of the sheriff or marshal. The marshal or sheriff will prepare a five-day notice to vacate and serve it or post it at the property. After five days, the marshal or sheriff will physically remove all tenants from the property. If this happens, try to get all your things moved before the sheriff or marshall comes. If you intend to leave behind personal property, see Chapter 12. California law does not allow a landlord to claim the proceeds from auctioning off the tenant's personal property unless he has a judgment. This would apply to back rent.

AFTER THE TRIAL: SPECIAL CONSIDERATIONS

TENANT'S
APPEAL

You have thirty days to file a notice of appeal. The appeal is to the appellate department of the superior court.

Our legal system allows one chance to bring a case to court. If you did not prepare for your trial, or thought you would not need a witness and you lost, you do not have the right to try again. However, in certain limited circumstances you may be able to have your case reviewed.

- If the judge made a mistake in interpreting the law that applies to your case, then that is grounds for reversal.

- If new evidence is discovered after the trial, which could not have been discovered before the trial, then a new trial might be granted, but this is not very common.

If one party lied at trial and that party was believed by the judge or jury, there is usually not much that can be done.

There are certain other grounds for rehearing such as misconduct of an attorney or errors during the trial, but these matters are beyond the scope of this book.

If you wish to appeal your case, you should consult with an attorney or review a book in the law library on California appellate practice.

A tenant's appeal does not necessarily delay eviction, unless the judge grants a stay, which is a postponement of any proceeding or judgement. If this is the case, the judgement of eviction is postponed and you deposit rent with the court.

FILING
BANKRUPTCY

If you file bankruptcy, all legal actions against you must stop immediately (called an *automatic stay*). This provision is automatic from the moment the bankruptcy petition is filed. If the landlord takes any action in court, seizes your property, tries to impose a landlord's lien, or uses the security deposit for unpaid rent, he can be held in contempt of federal court. It is not necessary that the landlord receive formal notice of the bankruptcy filing. Verbal notice is sufficient. The stay lasts until the debtor (you) is discharged or the case is dismissed, or until the property is abandoned or voluntarily surrendered.

The landlord may ask for the right to continue with the eviction by filing a Motion for Relief from Stay and paying the filing fee. Within thirty days a hearing is held, and it may be held by telephone. You can see how declaring bankruptcy can delay eviction even if you lose the unlawful detainer suit.

If you filed bankruptcy after a judgment of eviction has been entered, the landlord will have no problem lifting the automatic stay since you no longer have an interest in the property. The bankruptcy stay only applies to amounts owed to the landlord at the time of filing the bankruptcy. Therefore, the landlord can sue you for eviction and rent owed for any time period after the filing of the bankruptcy petition, unless the bankruptcy trustee assumes the lease. If this happens, all rents, past and future, become part of the bankruptcy.

The landlord can proceed during the bankruptcy without asking for relief from the automatic stay under three conditions:

1. The landlord can sue for rent due after the filing (not subject to the bankruptcy).

2. The landlord may sue after the trustee rejects the lease. (If the trustee does not accept the lease within sixty days of the Order for Relief, then it is deemed rejected.)

3. The landlord must sue under the terms of the lease and may not treat the trustee's rejection as a breach.

In a Chapter 13 (reorganization) bankruptcy, the landlord should be paid the rent as it comes due.

RESPONSIBLE RECORD-KEEPING

I have saved some advice for last because I believe it is the most important thing you will get out of the chapter and possibly out of this book.

The main reason that people lose lawsuits is poor record keeping. In order to prevent this, when you move in, take pictures and fill out the form to indicate any broken, worn or otherwise damaged parts of the property, appliances and furniture. Do the same thing when you move out.

Buy a notebook to be used only for your rental unit. Every time something goes wrong, whether it is a broken garbage disposal in your unit or trouble with your neighbor's dog, write it down with the date and time it happened and the date and time you talked to the landlord about it. Write the date, time and subject of any discussion you have with the landlord when you bring a problem to his attention.

Anytime you write to the landlord with a complaint, be sure to date your letter and keep a copy.

Whenever you contact anyone regarding a problem with your rental, write in the book the date, time, subject matter and person to whom you spoke. This is especially true of people at government offices. They may not want to give you their full name. At least get the first name and first letter of the last name. If you write to them, date the letter and keep a copy.

Buy a file folder (an oversized envelope will do) and keep all writings pertaining to the rental in this one place. This would include all rent checks, checks and receipts for repairs, copies of letters to and from the landlord and government agencies, and any other writing about rental problems.

There is nothing more impressive to your landlord, his attorney, and the court than having more than just your word against the landlord's. When the landlord says that you only complained once about a certain problem and you pull out your book and rattle off the four dates on which you complained, the landlord knows that he is in trouble. He knows that he cannot lie anymore or he is going to get caught. When you say that you called a government office on a certain date and talked to Shelly W., the court will listen. When you say you called but are not quite sure when and do not know to whom you spoke, you do not have much credibility.

If you hire a lawyer, she will have a great advantage in being able to see exactly what has been done and be better able to advise you. She will spend less time trying to figure out the facts of your case. This alone will save you a lot of money. She will also be able to tell you if you are wasting your time and money fighting the landlord about your particular problem. This could save you even more money.

NOTE: *Keeping good records is critical. Do not ignore this advice.*

TENANTS' ORGANIZATIONS 16

Tenants' organizations are formed because the individual tenant is often at a disadvantage when dealing with a landlord, especially an unscrupulous one. The landlord usually has more money and a greater knowledge of landlord/tenant law. As a group, tenants have a better chance to prevail in disputes. It can be compared to employees forming a union, which is why another name for a tenants' organization is a tenants' union. This chapter covers when and how to form a tenants' organization.

FORMING AN ORGANIZATION

Forming or joining a tenants' group is a serious matter and should be carefully thought out before action is taken.

First, be sure that your grievances are genuine. A good way to ascertain this is to talk to a cross-section of other tenants. If almost all believe that you are overreacting or being petty, reassess your position. You do this for two reasons. First, maybe they are right. If you are angry about some recent run-in with the landlord, give yourself a chance to cool off. Second, if most of the other tenants do not believe in your cause, you will not get much support. You will simply be considered a trouble maker.

Another situation to consider is when you are asked by other tenants to join a group. This can be a delicate situation. If you do not believe in their cause, you have to find a way to say no without getting them angry with you. Landlords are not the only ones who can retaliate against you. Try to determine if the group consists of only those who complain about everything or if there are reasonable people in the group who are genuinely aggrieved. Again, you may want to reassess your position and join.

Having said that, let us assume that you have genuine complaints, you have given the landlord every reasonable opportunity to correct the situation, and you know that stronger action is necessary. You have talked to other tenants and found many who agree with you. It is time to find strength in numbers.

INTERNET RESEARCH

The first thing to do is some research. The Internet has several sources. Use a search engine. I recommend a search engine rather than giving you specific websites. I have tried websites only to find that they no longer exist. Also, new sources are being added all the time and you will not find them if you are only trying specific web sites.

Type in "California tenants." You will find everything from lawyers who specialize in this area of the law to government agencies to tenant advocate groups that offer free counseling. Correspond with organizations (sometimes called associations or unions) in your area. Get a feel for the time and effort necessary to be effective. Doing this will not only help get you started, it will get you familiar with resources you may need later. Be sure that once you commit, you are willing to follow through.

SEEK ADVICE FROM AN ATTORNEY

I advise that you meet with a lawyer. You can get recommendations from your local bar association or tenant groups in your area. You may get a free first meeting, especially if the lawyer is already representing the tenant group that recommended her. Tell the lawyer what you are planning to do and ask what to expect. Also, if you are impressed with the lawyer, ask if she would represent your group. Be sure you tell her that you do not have authority to hire her but will recommend her to the group. Get a few of her business cards.

CALLING A
MEETING

Pick a convenient time and location. Personally talk to as many tenants as possible. Make up flyers even if you talk to all the tenants. Use the flyers as reminders. Post some in strategic places, such as near elevators and building entrances.

As soon as you call the meeting, your landlord will know about it. Several things may happen. The landlord may promise to change the situation that you are concerned with. Let us say you are worried about building safety. The landlord says that a security guard will be hired to patrol the grounds after dark. Let us also say that this satisfies you. Do you cancel the meeting? No. You tell the landlord that this is good news. If you get something in writing stating when the guard will start patrolling, you will be happy to read it to the other tenants at the meeting.

This now puts you in a good position. If you get something to read at the meeting, the other tenants will now know of the promise and be anxious to support any action you may suggest if the promise is not kept.

If the landlord refuses to give you, in writing or verbally, a specific date for the guard to start, you can tell this to the other tenants. This will confirm the need for the organization that you are trying to establish by showing that the landlord is not seriously addressing the problem.

Another possibility is that the landlord may ask to address the meeting. This creates an interesting situation. Usually a landlord does not ask this unless he feels that the tenants can be persuaded to drop the idea of a tenants' organization. My advice is to tell the landlord that you would rather that he not attend but will read any statement he gives you.

The first meeting should be simple. You want to have control of the meeting. You are not going to get much accomplished with the landlord there. Again, this probably will not happen but you should consider all possibilities.

If your meeting is in a place where the landlord has a right to be, you cannot keep him out. If it is in someone's apartment, you can.

Another possibility is that the landlord will threaten you with eviction. You might want to hand him one of your attorney's cards and tell him that this lawyer said that it is against the law to evict for that reason. The card is always more effective than just saying that your lawyer said something.

THE FIRST MEETING

The first meeting sets the tone for the group. Some will want only to complain. When it comes to doing something about it, they will not get involved. This is especially true if it costs them money. Others, even though they attend, will be reluctant to complain, fearing retaliation by the landlord. Some will want to see the plan before committing to action. If you do not run the meeting properly, you may not get a second chance.

INFORMAL INTRODUCTION

Even though the meeting should be informal, there should be some structure to it. You do not want people talking in small groups rather than addressing the entire group. This means that you must run the meeting.

If you are having the meeting at your apartment, do not get carried away with refreshments. Water and coffee should suffice. It is not a party.

Initially, you might ask if everyone knows each other and ask if people want to introduce themselves. Some may only want to observe and do not want to announce their presence.

Next, tell them something about tenants' rights organizations. Assure them that having this meeting and forming an organization to address their problems is protected by law from landlord retaliation. This is why I earlier suggested an attorney consultation. If someone challenges you (How do you know the law? Are you a lawyer?), you have an answer. You are letting them know that you do not say things you cannot back up. Credibility is most important if you want people to follow your lead.

PURPOSE OF MEETING

Explain the purpose of the meeting. State your concerns and ask for others to express their opinions or other problems. Make a list of the problems expressed to let the other tenants know that you are not just interested in your own complaints.

Try to get something accomplished beyond just airing grievances. A good start is to make up a name for your organization. An easy one is simply the property address followed by the word "organization" or "union." This is helpful for two reasons. First, everyone in the organization will remember it. Second, any mention of your organization will automatically identify the building. This could decrease applications to rent. The landlord will not want the publicity.

If you have made sufficient progress to get other tenants involved, start assigning jobs. You need to get a lawyer. You can ask if it is okay if you handle that since you have already had a consultation. You should know what the lawyer will charge per hour.

DEVELOP STRUCTURE OF ORGANIZATION

A member should be in charge of contacting and soliciting the experience of existing tenants' organizations. Since you have already done this, you can get her started. A member should keep a record of the group's members and be the contact for new membership.

FEES

A member should handle the group's finances. You should make sure everyone is aware that this will cost money, and should estimate how much. If any money is needed immediately, it should be asked for. New members should then be required to pay a fee to offset this. Some reimbursement can be made as more tenants join.

At this point you may encounter resistance. Some may refuse to pay. More commonly, some may promise to pay later and not. You will get a good idea of who is serious and the problems you may have covering expenses.

GATHER LANDLORD BACKGROUND INFORMATION

Knowing something about the landlord is important. If your landlord is a large company with plenty of money, a rent strike may not be your best option. Publicity may be a more effective. If your landlord is an individual struggling to have the rents cover the mortgage, a rent strike, or just the threat of one, may be a very powerful tool.

You can get the name of the owner from the county recorder's office or from a title company. It is easier from a title company. All you need is the address. If you have anyone in your group in the real estate business, banking, mortgage lending, appraisal, escrow, or any other business dealing with title companies, the information will be free. If not, you may have to pay a small fee. You can usually find someone in your group who knows someone who deals with title companies and will do you a favor. You can also check the tax records, but this will not necessarily give you the owner.

You can also have the title company check for liens against the property. This will not only include mortgages but tax liens and recorded judgments. This may give you an idea of the landlord's financial position.

If you have been dealing with a management company, you will want to contact the head of the company as well as the owner of the property. It is possible that they are not aware of the problems and will correct them. This is most effectively done with a letter from your attorney. Again, money will be a consideration.

IDENTIFY IMPORTANT CITY AND COUNTY OFFICES

You must have someone go to the city and county offices and talk to the various building and health departments. You need to know if they are aware of your problems and if they consider them serious enough to take action. Simply going to the information counter in major cities and counties will get you to the right departments. In small towns, it may all be in one department. When your member talks to the various people involved, she should tell them that you are attempting to get the landlord to correct the problems voluntarily. You just want to know where you stand if he refuses. Be sure she writes down who she talked to, when, and a summary of the conversation.

If your building is under rent control or any type of subsidized housing, find out where the local office is located and who runs it. Contact them and get their opinion on your problems.

You also want to have someone call the local newspaper and TV station to find out who covers this area of the news.

TRY TO WORK *WITH* THE LANDLORD

There is a logical order to this. You first do all the things to give the landlord a chance to correct the situation, such as contacting the head of the management company and the owner of record. If this does not work, ask your lawyer to write to the landlord asking for a meeting before further action is taken. This will result either in negotiations or a refusal to negotiate.

It also takes time and effort. You should set times at the first meeting to get progress reports from the various members doing this work and a time and place for a second meeting of the entire group. You do not want the enthusiasm you generated at the first meeting to fade with time.

THE SECOND MEETING

The second meeting will have one of three purposes.

- You may be just giving a progress report to the members. This will keep the group together and let them know you are working on the problem.

- You may use it as a barometer to gauge the success of the first meeting. If your first meeting went well, you will see some new members and a good turnout. If no one shows up, you know you are in trouble.

- The third purpose is planning the negotiations.

NEGOTIATION STRATEGY

You will plan your negotiating strategy. You may want someone from another tenants' group with negotiating experience to advise you. You may also want your attorney present to advise you as to what you can legally do if negotiations fail so you know what you can threaten to do at the negotiations.

If you have the support of a large number of tenants, you will want to negotiate in a large room and have as many members present as possible. If your numbers are rather small, you will tell the landlord that only the negotiating "team" will be present. Either way, you have to pick those people who will do the negotiating. You can ask the landlord if he wants attorneys present or you can simply tell him that your attorney will be present.

Check with your city and/or county to see if they have facilities and perhaps a mediator for this purpose. Do not meet at the landlord's office. You want neutral turf or your turf.

NOTE: *If you and the landlord agree not to have attorneys present and his shows up, demand that his attorney leave. If he refuses, you leave.*

NEGOTIATION GUIDELINES

Strategy for any negotiations have certain guidelines.

- You always start by asking for more than you are willing to accept. If you do not, you cannot compromise.

- Agree among your group on those issues that are crucial. In other words, the minimum that you are willing to accept and cannot settle for less.

- Write your list of demands and stick to talking about only those demands. You have to stay focused on what you want and not let the negotiations deteriorate into personal attacks or other matters.

TAKING ACTION

If the landlord refuses to negotiate, you will need to meet to plan your actions. Again, a representative from another tenants' group will be helpful. Your attorney will be necessary at this meeting since you are going to take actions and want to make sure they are legal.

Your research will now pay off. You should complain in writing to the appropriate government agencies. It is helpful if the complaints are on your attorney's letterhead.

You should decide if you want to picket. If you do, be sure that the media is notified well in advance. If you are considering a rent strike, you have already been advised by your attorney that the problems are serious enough to warrant this action.

Write a letter to the bank or to whomever has the mortgage on the property. State in the letter the violations that could impair the value of their security and let them know that you plan to withhold rent if they are not corrected. If the landlord has let the building deteriorate significantly, the lender has the right to call the loan. They usually do not but they can. Let them know that you feel that by not taking any action, they are contributing to the problem. Tell them that for this reason you are considering picketing their office, assuming that they have a local office to picket.

This may do you no good but if the lender puts pressure on the landlord, you have gained a powerful ally. You can also consider the possibility of a lawsuit.

SUCCESSFUL
AGREEMENT

If your group successfully negotiates an agreement, be sure that the *written agreement* is clearly stated. Put the legal description of the property on the agreement and have a notary present at the signing. Take the document to the county recorder's office and try to record it. Some offices may not accept the document for recording. Others will.

If you can record it, it gives notice to and binds future owners. If not, a future owner may not be bound by the agreement unless she is actually aware of it.

ROOMMATES, LODGERS, AND THE LAW

17

The difference between a roommate and a lodger is simple. A *roommate* shares a rental unit with another tenant. A *lodger* shares a unit with the owner. The law treats roommates and lodgers quite differently.

LODGERS

Let us start with a lodger. If you rent a room from the owner of a house, you are a lodger. The owner may refer to you as his roommate, but you are not legally equal. Section 1946.5 of the California civil code sets out the rule. The section reads as follows:

California Civil Code 1946.5. (a) The hiring of a room by a lodger on a periodic basis within a dwelling unit occupied by the owner may be terminated by either party giving written notice to the other of his or her intention to terminate the hiring, at least as long before the expiration of the term of the hiring as specified in Section 1946. The notice shall be given in a manner prescribed in Section 1162 of the Code of Civil Procedure or by certified or registered mail, restricted delivery, to the other party, with a return receipt requested. (b) Upon expiration of the notice period provided in the notice of termination given pursuant to subdivision (a), any right of the lodger to remain in the dwelling unit or any part thereof is terminated by operation of law. The lodger's removal from the premises may thereafter be effected pursuant to the provisions of Section 602.3 of the Penal Code or other applicable provisions of law. (c) As used in this section, "lodger" means a person contracting with the owner of a dwelling unit for a room or room and board within the dwelling unit personally occupied by the owner, where the owner retains a right of access to all areas of the dwelling unit occupied by the lodger and has overall control of the dwelling unit. (d) This section applies only to owner-occupied dwellings where a single lodger resides. Nothing in this section shall be construed to determine or affect in any way the rights of persons residing as lodgers in an owner-occupied dwelling where more than one lodger resides.

The reference to Section 602.3 of the Penal Code means that if you stay beyond the time of your notice, the owner does not have to file an action for Unlawful Detainer. He can go to the police, show them the notice, and they will come and remove you from the property. Section 602.3 reads as follows:

California Penal Code Section 602.3. (a) A lodger who is subject to Section 1946.5 of the Civil Code and who remains on the premises of an owner-occupied dwelling unit after receipt of a notice terminating the hiring, and expiration of the notice period, provided in Section 1946.5 of the Civil Code is guilty of an infraction and may, pursuant to Section 837, be arrested for the offense by the owner, or in the event the owner is represented by a court-appointed conservator, executor, or administrator, by the owner's representative. Notwithstanding Section 853.5, the requirement of that section for release upon a written promise to appear shall not preclude an assisting peace officer from removing the person from the owner-occupied dwelling unit. (b) The removal of a lodger from a dwelling unit by the owner pursuant to subdivision (a) is not a forcible entry under the provisions of Section 1159 of the Code of Civil Procedure and shall not be a basis for civil liability under that section. (c) Chapter 5 (commencing with Section 1980) of Title 5 of Part 4 of Division 3 of the Civil Code applies to any personal property of the lodger which remains on the premises following the lodger's removal from the premises pursuant to this section. (d) Nothing in this section shall be construed to limit the owner's right to have a lodger removed under other provisions of law. (e) Except as provided in subdivision (b), nothing in this section shall be construed to limit or affect in any way any cause of action an owner or lodger may have for damages for any breach of the contract of the parties respecting the lodging. (f) This section applies only to owner-occupied dwellings where a single lodger resides. Nothing in this section shall be construed to determine or affect in any way the rights of persons residing as lodgers in an owner-occupied dwelling where more than one lodger resides.

As you can see, it is easy for the owner to throw you out after the notice period. I am sure you also noticed that if there is more than one lodger, the section does not apply.

ROOMMATES

You acquire roommates in two ways.

- You and another person (or persons) sign a lease or rental agreement (or make an oral one) with a landlord.

- Someone moves in with you *after* you have signed your rental agreement.

SIGN LEASE
TOGETHER

You are equally responsible to the landlord for all the rent and liable for any damage to the unit. It is just as if you are there by yourself. You cannot blame anything on your roommate to relieve your obligations.

Landlords frequently hear that the reason the rent is unpaid or the unit was damaged was the fault of the roommate. Although this may be true, it means nothing. If your roommate's check bounces or her friend damages the property, you are responsible just as much as she. Not for half the amount, but for the total.

So, what is the first rule? Be selective. Be sure that your roommate is a responsible person. Make certain that she has a sufficient legal source of income to cover rent and unexpected expenses.

It is not unreasonable to get a credit report. This can be done quickly and cheaply, either from a credit bureau or a company that will get it for you from all three major credit bureaus. If you see a history of unpaid debt or a judgment for back rent from a previous landlord, you will avoid what could be a very costly relationship.

Should you sign a lease or rental agreement? If you sign, for example, a one-year lease and your roommate moves out after two months, you may have a problem paying the rent. You can see the advantage of a month-to-month agreement.

Next draw an agreement between you and your roommate. Set out each of your responsibilities. This is especially important if you are not sharing costs equally. Perhaps, for example, you travel frequently for your job and will only be paying one third of the utilities because of this. Also, one of you will usually write the checks and collect from the other, especially for utilities and maybe even for rent. Put the procedure in your agreement.

Always set out responsibility for the phone bill. I recommend that you get separate phones. Although you and your roommate are equally responsible to the landlord, you have rights against each other. If your roommate causes damage or fails to pay her share of the rent, you can sue her for the cost involved. The problem is collection. Picking a responsible roommate is more important than all the legal remedies available to you.

Temperament is also frequently overlooked. If your roommate is someone who enjoys confrontation and is going to complain about every minor annoyance caused by the landlord or other tenants, you may find yourself embroiled in disputes that you consider petty. A "perfectionist" can be a difficult roommate.

AFTER LEASE
HAS BEEN
SIGNED

The second way to acquire a roommate is having someone move in with you after you have signed your lease or rental agreement.

This may or may not require the landlord's consent, depending on your contract with him. If it does, he may give consent as required (usually in writing) or may give implied consent by accepting rent from your roommate.

If you and your roommate sign a new agreement, your obligations are as described above. If not, your roommate has no contractual relationship with the landlord. Your responsibilities remain the same.

If your lease or rental agreement specifically prohibits subletting and bringing in roommates, it is enforceable. The only time such a subletting prohibition is void is when you move out, based on the landlord's duty to mitigate, as discussed in Chapter 6.

If you do not sign a new agreement, you must collect rent and any other agreed upon expenses from your roommate. She is liable to both you and the landlord for any damages she causes but the landlord will probably go after you rather than her. He knows you are good for it. If your roommate decides to move out, it is no problem. If you decide to move out and have her take your place, it is a different situation.

If it is a month-to-month agreement, you simply write or tell the landlord of this when you give your thirty-day notice that you are leaving. Since the notice is in writing, make the request in writing.

Your landlord may then want an application and credit report before deciding, but that is not your problem. It is just as if your roommate was applying for the rental. The rent may be increased and she will have to pay a security deposit, or your landlord may reject her and she will have to move.

NOTE: *In rent controlled areas, if the landlord has accepted rent directly from your roommate, she may have greater rights.*

If you have a lease that has not yet expired, you will be in the same situation as if you were in the unit by yourself and decided to move out early. You are counting on mitigation of damages. If your roommate has a sufficient legal source of income and good credit, you should not have a problem. If not, the landlord could reject her and you may be liable for the unpaid balance of the lease unless an acceptable tenant can be found.

GUESTS

Many agreements specify the number of days that a guest may stay before being considered to be living in the unit. If it is not covered, it is a judgment call except in the extreme situation. One night or even one week would obviously be a guest. One year would obviously be someone living in the unit.

For example, having someone stay for two weeks, then move out for a day and then back in for another two weeks would be viewed as a four-week continuous stay unless you could show some very unusual circumstance to justify it. In other words, the court would look at your intent. If the court believes that your intent was only to avoid violating the clause in your lease or rental agreement, you will not get away with it. If, according to the clause in your lease or rental agreement, four weeks continuous occupancy changes the status from guest to someone who is living in the unit, you have violated the clause.

If you expect frequent guests, ask for the landlord's policy before you rent if it is not spelled out to your satisfaction in the agreement.

SELF-STORAGE FACILITIES 18

When real property is rented for the storage of personal property and not as a residence, different legal rules apply. This is understandable since you are not dealing with people (tenants) but with things. The landlord does not, for example, have to make the premises habitable (fit for people to live in). Landlords also do not have the leverage of eviction. The tenant is not losing a place to live. The rules are generally more favorable to the landlord in comparison to the rules for renting to people.

APPLICABILITY

The rental of space in self-storage facilities is controlled by the California Business and Professions Code, beginning with Section 21700.

A self-storage facility is real property used to store personal property. It is not a warehouse nor a garage or other part of a private residence and it cannot be used as a residence.

If you rented out a garage separately, and not as part of a residence rental, it could qualify as a self-storage facility.

Rental Agreement

In addition to the occupant's name and address, the rental agreement must also have a space for the occupant to provide an alternative address (although the occupant is not required to give one). If the landlord wishes to have the ability to sell the stored property in order to satisfy unpaid rent, it must be stated in the agreement.

Termination for Unpaid Rent

If the rent is unpaid for fourteen days, the landlord may terminate the agreement by sending a notice to the occupant's (tenant's) last known address and the alternative address, if any, given in the rental agreement.

Liens

A lien is a legal right or interest that a creditor has to their debtor's property and serves as protection in case the debtor does not pay back the creditor as initially promised. The owner of a self-storage facility is like a "creditor," and has a lien for rent, labor, or other charges on the property stored in the unit. It does not matter whose property it is; the lien attaches to any property in the unit on the date it is brought to the facility.

The lien on a vehicle or vessel is subject to prior liens. In other words, if the car or boat is not free and clear, that lien takes priority over the storage lien.

The California Business and Professional Code sets forth the instructions for how the lien sale is to be carried out, and even includes the forms that should be sent to the occupant. A copy of the PRELIMINARY LIEN NOTICE is included as form 33 in Appendix C of this book.

CONCLUSION 19

CHECKLISTS

You should have two checklists. One should be for **things to do** and the other should be for **things to ask**.

To Do
- ❏ Measure the unit if you have any doubt about fitting in your furniture.

- ❏ Note the number and size of closets. Closet space is often overlooked.

- ❏ Check at least a few of the electrical outlets as well as light switches. This may require bringing something small, like a shaver or hair dryer, with you. If you have a tester, even better.

- ❏ Check water pressure. Turn on the tap or shower in the bathroom and then flush the toilet. See if the water from the faucet or shower slows significantly.

- ❏ Try the garbage disposal.

- ❏ Check under the sinks in the kitchen and bath for water damage and mold.

- ❏ Turn on the heater and air conditioner for a few minutes.

❒ Check all windows for cracks and be sure they all lock properly and have undamaged screens.

❒ If there are blinds or curtains, be sure the blinds work and the curtains have no stains or tears.

❒ Be sure the doors open and close easily.

❒ Try all door locks. You should not have to force them open or closed.

❒ Check walls, ceilings, and floors for cracks or signs of water damage.

❒ If the unit is furnished, check the furniture and also check behind the furniture for damaged walls and carpeting.

❒ If there is a balcony, check the railing and the space between the vertical slats (could a child get stuck between them?).

❒ Checking the parking area and neighborhood are discussed in detail in Chapter 1.

❒ Any damage should be noted and, if not going to be repaired, photographed. Use the INSPECTION REPORT in Appendix C will most likely be similar to the one the landlord will use. (see form 3, p.145.) I suggest that you use a notebook that you keep for all things associated with the rental. Write the date, the room and the damage, such as: June 12, 2003, living room, worn carpeting leading to hall. Sometimes worn carpeting can be difficult to photograph so your notation will be what you submit to a court if there is a dispute over the security deposit. If you keep good records, a court will find you very credible.

To Ask

☐ Rent increases – How often and how much is usual?

☐ How long has the landlord owned the property? (New owners usually raise the rent.)

☐ Are there any costs above the rent, such as shared utilities?

☐ If there is a "clubhouse," can it be reserved for private parties? Free? How often?

☐ Are any improvements planned? (Another reason to increase the rent.)

☐ Is any work planned for your unit before you move in (new paint carpet,etc.)?

☐ Have there been problems with security (break-ins or assaults)? If so, what precautions are now in place?

☐ Have there been problems with other tenants that would make you want to avoid them?

☐ How safe is the neighborhood?

☐ Is the landlord aware of the quality of local schools?

☐ Where are the schools, churches, and shopping?

☐ You should, of course, check things out on your own, like visiting the local school, church, and shopping center.

GLOSSARY

A

actual damages.   Money lost by the plaintiff due to the wrongful acts of the defendant. This differs from other types of damages such as *punitive* or *liquidated*.

agent.   One who acts on behalf of another (called the *principal*) with authority to commit the principal to a contract.

assignment.   A transfer of rights, such as those of a lease. The person receiving the rights is called the assignee; the one transferring the rights is called the assignor. A transfer of duties is called a delegation.

B

back rent.   Commonly describes rent that is more than one rental period in arrears, although it can mean any unpaid rent that is due.

bad faith.   Acting with intent to do wrong rather than simply making a mistake.

breach.   Violating the terms of a contract without a legal excuse.

buried clauses.   Clauses in a contract that are difficult to find unless the contract is read very carefully. The law requires certain clauses to be in a specific size or bold type or to be located in an easy to see place, such as just above where the parties will sign.

C

causation.   A necessary element to collect damages. The plaintiff must show that the defendant's conduct caused the damages to the plaintiff.

complaint.   The initial filing of a lawsuit. The plaintiff files the complaint alleging the reason for the suit and the defendant then must file an answer.

contempt of court.   Violation of a court order or improper behavior in a courtroom.

cosigner.   One who signs to secure the debt of another. The cosigner is just as liable as the debtor unless otherwise agreed.

court hearing.   A general term covering any number of court proceedings. It differs from a trial in that there is no jury and may be based on legal, rather than factual, issues.

credit report.   A history of the debts of a person with emphasis on whether the debts were paid as agreed. The report is commonly used by prospective lenders, landlords, and employers.

curable breach.   A violation of a contract that can be corrected. A landlord can send a notice to a tenant demanding that the tenant correct the violation of the lease before beginning eviction.

D

damages.   The financial harm done to the defendant. Examples could be the tenant's failure to pay the rent or physical damage to the property.

default.   Failure to fulfill an obligation, rather than actively doing something wrong. Failure to pay rent is the most common.

defendant index.   A list of cases filed by the name of the defendant. This lets the researcher see all the cases filed in the past against a particular person.

deposition.   Questioning a witness outside the courtroom. The witness may have an attorney, but rules of questioning are not as strict as in court questioning.

discovery.   The giving of information to the opposing side in a lawsuit. Modern legal theory is that surprises are less likely to produce a just result than openness. A criminal defendant does not, of course, have to give incriminating information to a prosecutor, but a prosecutor must give exculpatory information to a defendant.

duty to mitigate.   The obligation of the plaintiff to hold damages to a minimum. An example is a landlord's obligation to try to re-rent the property after a tenant moves out before the lease ends.

E

eviction.   The process of removing a person from property.

F

fictitious name.   A name other than the name of the person. It does not have to be for a wrongful purpose. For example, Joe Smith owns his building in the name of Smith's Resort.

G

garnishment.   The taking of a person's wages to pay a debt. There must first be a judgment against the person and there are rules as to the procedures to follow and the maximum that can be taken from a pay period.

guarantor.   One who agrees to be liable for the debt of another. A guarantor of payment is liable the same as the debtor (*primary liability*). A guarantor of collection is liable only after the creditor has been unable to collect from the debtor (*secondary liability*).

guaranty.   Agreeing to be liable for the debt of another.

H

habitability.   A condition fit for human occupancy. A landlord has a duty to have the rental unit fit for the tenant to live in, such as having heat and working plumbing. This is a minimum standard required by law. The standard agreed to by the parties may be much higher.

I

implied authorization.   Authority of an agent implied by his or her position, even if there is no actual authority. If a building manager, for example, collects rent against the wishes of the owner, but the owner has not informed the tenant that the manager has no authority to do this, the tenant is not responsible for any loss suffered by the owner if the manager keeps the money.

incurable breach.   A violation of a contract that is so severe the landlord simply wants the tenant out of the residence.

injunction.   A remedy to prevent a person from doing something, rather than collecting damages for the harm caused. If you want the factory next to your building to stop emitting noxious fumes, you could sue for an injunction to make it stop.

intentional acts.   Those acts that are deliberately done. Intentional wrongdoing is generally considered more serious than carelessness (negligence) or acts for which one is strictly liable.

interest (as in an interest in property).   A right in property. It may be the right of an owner, the right to occupy as a tenant, or some lesser right as to travel across the property (easement right).

interest-bearing account.   An account earning money simply for being in the account. Some money held by a landlord, such as security deposits, may be placed in such accounts.

interrogatories.   Questions submitted by parties to a lawsuit to the opposing side. They are in written form, rather than verbal questions, as in a deposition.

J

judgment.   The decision of a court. It will determine if the plaintiff is entitled to damages (if the plaintiff won) and how much the damages are.

just cause.   A legal and lawful reason to bring a legal action.

L

landlord.   An owner of property who rents the property to a tenant.

landlord/tenant law.   That portion of Real Property Law dealing with the legal relationship between an owner of property (landlord) and one who rents the property (tenant).

lease.   A contract between a landlord and a tenant setting forth the rights and duties agreed to by each. It differs from a rental agreement in that it has a definite termination date.

levy.   A collection, seizure, or assessment.

liability.   Legal responsibility to do, or refrain from doing something. This means you can be sued (be liable) for failure to carry out this responsibility.

liens.   Money encumbrances against property. Examples would be mortgages or deeds of trust (voluntary liens) or judgments and tax liens (involuntary liens).

liquidated damages.   A preset estimate of damages should the contract be breached, when actual damages would be difficult to determine. Common in real estate sales contracts. For example, the buyer loses the deposit if he breaches the contract (does not go through with the sale). The amount must be reasonable or it will be considered a penalty and, therefore, void.

M

management company.   A business that takes care of property for the owner. It may be responsible for collecting rents, maintenance, leasing to and evicting tenants, or all of these.

N

negligence.   Failure to use reasonable care by one who has a duty to do so. The failure must cause damages to the plaintiff. If a landlord, for example, fails to use reasonable care to keep a building safe (make repairs, for instance), and this failure causes injury to a tenant, the landlord would be liable for negligence.

negligence per se.   Negligence from violating a statute (law). For example, if the law says that you must have a fence around your pool and you do not, injury caused by not having the fence would be negligence per se.

notary.   One who is licensed by the state to attest to the authenticity of a signature. In order to have almost all documents recorded, the signature on the document must be notarized.

notice.   Informing of something that has happened or is going to happen. Recording a deed, for example, would give notice that a transfer of ownership has taken place. A notice to quit would tell the tenant to move within a given time in the future.

notice to quit.   Informing a tenant to leave the property or face eviction. The notice could simply demand that the tenant leave or be conditional, such as pay the rent owed or leave.

O

on-site manager.   A person who lives on the property and is responsible for the day-to-day activities, such as collection of rent, maintenance, and showing the property to prospective tenants.

option.   The choice of entering into a contract. For example, a lease could give the tenant the option (right but not obligation) to extend beyond the expiration date or the option to purchase the property.

ordinances.   County and city laws. They are called statutes at the state or federal level.

P

punitive damages.   Money the defendant must pay as a punishment or to set an example (also called exemplary damages) for especially bad behavior. Requires more than simple breach or negligence.

R

reasonable care.   The care a reasonably prudent person would take under the circumstances. Failure to use reasonable care is required to prove negligence.

rent.   The periodic payment of money in exchange for the right to possession of the property.

rent control.   Governmental regulations setting maximum rents and rules for eviction beyond normal contract law.

rent control board.   A group that monitors and enforces rent control.

rescission.   Returning the parties to a contract to their positions before the contract. This may not always be possible as the subject matter of the contract cannot always be returned.

retaliatory evictions.   Demanding a tenant leave in response to a legitimate action taken by the tenant, such as reporting the landlord for health code violations. If the eviction is considered retaliatory, it is illegal.

right of first refusal.   Giving a tenant the right to match any offer to buy the property. The tenant must "first refuse" to buy before the owner can sell to a third party.

S

safe-harbor rule. Any rule considered within the law or disclaimers to avoid liability.

screening. Checking the background of a prospective tenant. This may include a credit report, verification of employment, reference of a prior landlord, etc.

security deposit. Money deposited with the landlord, in addition to rent, to be used if the tenant fails to pay the agreed upon rent or causes damage to the property.

service of process. The delivery of the paperwork necessary to begin a lawsuit. A landlord must inform tenants where service of process can be received.

standard of care. How much a person must do to avoid damage to another to whom a duty is owed. The law sets minimum standards for a landlord's operation of a rental property for the health and safety of the tenant. The standard may be raised by agreement of the parties or promises by the landlord.

statutes. Laws passed by the federal congress or state legislators. County and city laws are called ordinances.

stay. A court order to stop a legal process in progress. For example, a bankruptcy court could stay (stop) an eviction or foreclosure proceeding. The owner or lender would then have to ask the court to lift the stay (grant a relief of stay).

stipulation. Agreement between the parties to a legal dispute on a specific point. This eliminates the need to prove the point.

strict liability. Holding one responsible for damages even though reasonable care was used to prevent the damage or injury. The plaintiff must still show that the defendant owed a duty to the plaintiff and that the plaintiff's actions caused the damages.

sublease. A lease between a tenant and a third party (subtenant). Subleasing is allowed unless the lease specifically prohibits it. Usually the lease states that approval of the landlord is required.

T

tenant. One who rents real property. The tenant receives the right to occupy the property in exchange for the payment of money (rent).

U

unconscionable clause. A clause in a contract that is so unfair (although not against the law) that a court cannot in good conscience enforce it. The clause must be unfair at the formation of the contract and the court can choose to enforce the rest of the contract.

unlawful detainer. The name for the legal action to evict someone from property.

W

waiver. The giving up of a right. For example, accepting late rent without charging the agreed upon late charge may be a waiver of future right to the late charge.

Z

zoning. The specified allowable use of property as set forth by county or city ordinance, or by master plan.

Appendix A
California
Landlord/Tenant
Statutes

The following California landlord/tenant statutes are for reference if you would like to read the exact statute that sets forth what your landlord *can and cannot legally do.* These statutes cover the following: how a landlord may legally establish rental rates; information that your landlord must tell you about your rental unit; terms your landlord must include in your rental agreement; changing terms in your lease; and, the kind of notice you are legally entitled to receive in the above situations.

Civil Code Section 1946: Notice Required to Terminate Tenancy

A hiring of real property, for a term not specified by the parties, is deemed to be renewed as stated in Section 1945, at the end of the term implied by law unless one of the parties gives written notice to the other of his intention to terminate the same, at least as long before the expiration thereof as the term of the hiring itself, not exceeding 30 days; provided, however, that as to tenancies from month to month either of the parties may terminate the same by giving at least 30 days' written notice thereof at any time and the rent shall be due and payable to and including the date of termination. It shall be competent for the parties to provide by an agreement at the time such tenancy is created that a notice of the intention to terminate the same may be given at any time not less than seven days before the expiration of the term thereof. The notice herein required shall be given in the manner pre-

scribed in Section 1162 of the Code of Civil Procedure or by sending a copy by certified or registered mail addressed to the other party. In addition, the lessee may give such notice by sending a copy by certified or registered mail addressed to the agent of the lessor to whom the lessee has paid the rent for the month prior to the date of such notice or by delivering a copy to the agent personally.

(a) Except as provided in subdivision (b), in all leases of lands or tenements, or of any interest therein, from week to week, month to month, or other period less than a month, the landlord may, upon giving notice in writing to the tenant, in the manner prescribed by Section 1162 of the Code of Civil Procedure, change the terms of the lease to take effect, as to tenancies for less than one month, upon the expiration of a period at least as long as the term of the hiring itself, and, as to tenancies from month to month, to take effect at the expiration of not less than 30 days, but if that change takes effect within a rental term, the rent accruing from the first day of the term to the date of that change shall be computed at the rental rate which obtained immediately prior to that change; provided, however, that it shall be competent for the parties to provide by an agreement in writing that a notice changing the terms thereof may be given at any time not less than seven days before the expiration of a term, to be effective upon the expiration of the term. The notice, when served upon the tenant, shall of itself operate and be effectual to create and establish, as a part of the lease, the terms, rents, and conditions specified in the notice, if the tenant shall continue to hold the premises after the notice takes effect.

(b) (1) In all leases of a residential dwelling, or of any interest therein, from week to week, month to month, or other period less than a month, the landlord may increase the rent provided in the lease or rental agreement, upon giving written notice to the tenant, as follows, by either of the following procedures:

(A) By delivering a copy to the tenant personally.

(B) By serving a copy by mail under the procedures prescribed in Section 1013 of the Code of Civil Procedure.

(2) If the proposed rent increase for that tenant is 10 percent or less of the rental amount charged to that tenant at any time during the 12 months prior to the effective date of the increase, either in and of itself or when combined with any other rent increases for the 12 months prior to the effective date of the increase, the notice shall be delivered at least 30 days prior to the effective date of the increase, and subject to Section 1013 of the Code of Civil Procedure if served by mail.

(3) For an increase in rent greater than the amount described in paragraph (2), the minimum notice period required pursuant to that paragraph shall be increased by an additional 30 days, and subject to Section 1013 of the Code of Civil Procedure if served by mail. This paragraph shall not apply to

an increase in rent caused by a change in a tenant's income or family composition as determined by a recertification required by statute or regulation.

(c) If a state or federal statute, state or federal regulation, recorded regulatory agreement, or contract provides for a longer period of notice regarding a rent increase than that provided in subdivision (a) or (b), the personal service or mailing of the notice shall be in accordance with the longer period.

(d) This section shall be operative only until January 1, 2006, and as of that date is repealed, unless a later enacted statute, which is enacted on or before January 1, 2006, deletes or extends that date.

Civil Code Section 827: Changes in Terms of Lease; Notice

(a) In all leases of lands or tenements, or of any interest therein, from week to week, month to month, or other period less than a month, the landlord may, upon giving notice in writing to the tenant, in the manner prescribed by Section 1162 of the Code of Civil Procedure, change the terms of the lease to take effect, as to tenancies for less than one month, upon the expiration of a period at least as long as the term of the hiring itself, and, as to tenancies from month to month, to take effect at the expiration of not less than 30 days, but if that change takes effect within a rental term, the rent accruing from the first day of the term to the date of that change shall be computed at the rental rate which was obtained immediately prior to that change; provided, however, that it shall be competent for the parties to provide by an agreement in writing that a notice changing the terms thereof may be given at any time not less than seven days before the expiration of a term, to be effective upon the expiration of the term. The notice, when served upon the tenant, shall of itself operate and be effectual to create and establish, as a part of the lease, the terms, rents, and conditions specified in the notice, if the tenant shall continue to hold the premises after the notice takes effect.

(b) This section shall become operative on January 1, 2006.

Code of Civil Procedure Section 1013: Proof of Service by Mail

(a) In case of service by mail, the notice or other paper shall be deposited in a post office, mailbox, subpost office, substation, or mail chute, or other like facility regularly maintained by the United States Postal Service, in a sealed envelope, with postage paid, addressed to the person on whom it is to be served, at the office address as last given by that person on any document filed in the cause and served on the party making service by mail; otherwise at that party's place of residence. The service is complete at the time of the deposit, but any period of notice and any right or duty to do any act or make any response within any period or on a date certain after the service of the document, which time period or date is prescribed by statute or rule of court, shall be extended five calendar days, upon service by mail, if the place of address and the place of mailing is within the State of California, 10 calendar days if either the place of mailing or the place of address is outside the State of California but within the United States, and 20 calendar days if either the place of mailing or the place of address is outside the United States, but the extension shall not apply to extend the time for filing notice of intention to move for new trial, notice of intention to move to vacate judgment pursuant to Section 663a, or notice of appeal. This extension applies in the absence of a specific exception provided for by this section or other statute or rule of court.

(b) The copy of the notice or other paper served by mail pursuant to this chapter shall bear a notation of the date and place of mailing or be accompanied by an unsigned copy of the affidavit or certificate of mailing.

(c) In case of service by Express Mail, the notice or other paper must be deposited in a post office, mailbox, subpost office, substation, or mail chute, or other like facility regularly maintained by the United States Postal Service for receipt of Express Mail, in a sealed envelope, with Express Mail postage paid, addressed to the person on whom it is to be served, at the office address as last given by that person on any document filed in the cause and served on the party making service by Express Mail; otherwise at that party's place of residence. In case of service by another method of delivery providing for overnight delivery, the notice or other paper must be deposited in a box or other facility regularly maintained by the express service carrier, or delivered to an authorized courier or driver authorized by the express service carrier to receive documents, in an envelope or package designated by the express service carrier with delivery fees paid or provided for, addressed to the person on whom it is to be served, at the office address as last given by that person on any document filed in the cause and served on the party making service; otherwise at that party' s place of residence. The service is complete at the time of the deposit, but any period of notice and any right or duty to do any act or make any response within any period or on a date certain after the service of the document served by Express Mail or other method of delivery providing for overnight delivery shall be extended by two court days, but the extension shall not apply to extend the time for filing notice of intention to move for new trial, notice of intention to move to vacate judgment pursuant to Section 663a, or notice of appeal. This extension applies in the absence of a specific exception provided for by this section or other statute or rule of court.

(d) The copy of the notice or other paper served by Express Mail or another means of delivery providing for overnight delivery pursuant to this chapter shall bear a notation of the date and place of deposit or be accompanied by an unsigned copy of the affidavit or certificate of deposit.

(e) Service by facsimile transmission shall be permitted only where the parties agree and a written confirmation of that agreement is made. The Judicial Council may adopt rules implementing the service of documents by facsimile transmission and may provide a form for the confirmation of the agreement required by this subdivision. In case of service by facsimile transmission, the notice or other paper must be transmitted to a facsimile machine maintained by the person on whom it is served at the facsimile machine telephone number as last given by that person on any document which he or she has filed in the cause and served on the party making the service. The service is complete at the time of transmission, but any period of notice and any right or duty to do any act or make any response within any period or on a date certain after the service of the document, which time period or date is prescribed by statute or rule of court, shall be extended, after service by facsimile transmission, by two court days, but the extension shall not apply to extend the time for filing notice of intention to move for new trial, notice of intention to move to vacate judgment pursuant to Section 663a, or notice of appeal. This extension applies in the absence of a specific exception provided for by this section or other statute or rule of court.

(f) The copy of the notice or other paper served by facsimile transmission pursuant to this chapter shall bear a notation of the date and place of transmission and the facsimile telephone number to which transmitted or be accompanied by an unsigned copy of the affidavit or certificate of transmission which shall contain the facsimile telephone number to which the notice or other paper was transmitted. (g) Subdivisions (b), (d), and (f) are directory.

Code of Civil Procedure Section 1162: Service of Notice

The notices required by sections 1161 and 1161a may be served, either: 1. By delivering a copy to the tenant personally; or, 2. If he be absent from his place of residence, and from his usual place of business, by leaving a copy with some person of suitable age and discretion at either place, and sending a copy through the mail addressed to the tenant at his place of residence; or, 3. If such place of residence and business can not be ascertained, or a person of suitable age or discretion there can not be found, then by affixing a copy in a conspicuous place on the property, and also delivering a copy to a person there residing, if such person can be found; and also sending a

copy through the mail addressed to the tenant at the place where the property is situated. Service upon a subtenant may be made in the same manner.

Civil Code Section 1954.52: Conditions for Owner to Establish Rental Rates

(a) Notwithstanding any other provision of law, an owner of residential real property may establish the initial and all subsequent rental rates for a dwelling or a unit about which any of the following is true:

(1) It has a certificate of occupancy issued after February 1, 1995.

(2) It has already been exempt from the residential rent control ordinance of a public entity on or before February 1, 1995, pursuant to a local exemption for newly constructed units.

(3) (A) It is alienable separate from the title to any other dwelling unit or is a subdivided interest in a subdivision, as specified in subdivision (b), (d), or (f) of Section 11004.5 of the Business and Professions Code.

(B) This paragraph does not apply to either of the following:

(i) A dwelling or unit where the preceding tenancy has been terminated by the owner by notice pursuant to Section 1946 or has been terminated upon a change in the terms of the tenancy noticed pursuant to Section 827.

(ii) A condominium dwelling or unit that has not been sold separately by the subdivider to a bona fide purchaser for value. The initial rent amount of such a unit for purposes of this chapter shall be the lawful rent in effect on May 7, 2001, unless the rent amount is governed by a different provision of this chapter. However, if a condominium dwelling or unit meets the criteria of paragraph (1) or (2) of subdivision (a), or if all the dwellings or units except one have been sold separately by the subdivider to bona fide purchasers for value, and the subdivider has occupied that remaining unsold condominium dwelling or unit as his or her principal residence for at least one year after the subdivision occurred, then subparagraph (A) of paragraph (3) shall apply to that unsold condominium dwelling or unit.

(C) Where a dwelling or unit in which the initial or subsequent rental rates are controlled by an ordinance or charter provision in effect on January 1, 1995, the following shall apply:

(i) An owner of real property as described in this paragraph may establish the initial and all subsequent rental rates for all existing and new tenancies in effect on or after January 1, 1999, if the tenancy in effect on or after January 1, 1999, was created between January 1, 1996, and December 31, 1998.

(ii) Commencing on January 1, 1999, an owner of real property as described in this paragraph may establish the initial and all subsequent rental rates for all new tenancies if the previous tenancy was in effect on December 31, 1995.

(iii) The initial rental rate for a dwelling or unit as described in this paragraph in which the initial rental rate is controlled by an ordinance or charter provision in effect on January 1, 1995, may not, until January 1, 1999, exceed the amount calculated pursuant to subdivision (c) of Section 1954.53. An owner of residential real property as described in this paragraph may, until January 1, 1999, establish the initial rental rate for a dwelling or unit only where the tenant has voluntarily vacated, abandoned, or been evicted pursuant to paragraph (2) of Section 1161 of the Code of Civil Procedure.

(b) Subdivision (a) does not apply where the owner has otherwise agreed by contract with a public entity in consideration for a direct financial contribution or any other forms of assistance specified in Chapter 4.3 (commencing with Section 65915) of Division 1 of Title 7 of the Government Code.

(c) Nothing in this section shall be construed to affect the authority of a public entity that may otherwise exist to regulate or monitor the basis for eviction.

(d) This section does not apply to any dwelling or unit that contains serious health, safety, fire, or building code violations, excluding those caused by disasters, for which a citation has been issued by the appropriate governmental agency and which has remained unabated for six months or longer preceding the vacancy.

Civil Code Section 1962(a): Information Required in Rental Agreement

(a) Any owner of a dwelling structure specified in Section 1961 or a party signing a rental agreement or lease on behalf of the owner shall do all of the following:

(1) Disclose therein the name, telephone number, and usual street address at which personal service may be effected of each person who is:

(A) Authorized to manage the premises.

(B) An owner of the premises or a person who is authorized to act for and on behalf of the owner for the purpose of service of process and for the purpose of receiving and receipting for all notices and demands.

(2) Disclose therein the name, telephone number, and address of the person or entity to whom rent payments shall be made.

(A) If rent payments may be made personally, the usual days and hours that the person will be available to receive the payments shall also be disclosed.

(B) At the owner's option, the rental agreement or lease shall instead disclose the number of either:

(i) The account in a financial institution into which rent payments may be made, and the name and street address of the institution; provided that the institution is located within five miles of the rental property.

(ii) The information necessary to establish an electronic funds transfer procedure for paying the rent.

(3) Disclose therein the form or forms in which rent payments are to be made.

(4) Provide a copy of the rental agreement or lease to the tenant within 15 days of its execution by the tenant. Once each calendar year thereafter, upon request by the tenant, the owner or owner's agent shall provide an additional copy to the tenant within 15 days. If the owner or owner's agent does not possess the rental agreement or lease or a copy of it, the owner or owner's agent shall instead furnish the tenant with a written statement stating that fact and containing the information required by paragraphs (1), (2), and (3) of subdivision (a).

Civil Code Section 1962.5: Alternate Methods of Disclosing Information

(a) Notwithstanding subdivisions (a) and (b) of Section 1962, the information required by paragraph (1) of subdivision (a) of Section 1962 to be disclosed to a tenant may, instead of being disclosed in the manner described in subdivisions (a) and (b) of Section 1962, be disclosed by the following method:

(1) In each dwelling structure containing an elevator a printed or typewritten notice containing the information required by paragraph (1) of subdivision (a) of Section 1962 shall be placed in every elevator and in one other conspicuous place.

(2) In each structure not containing an elevator, a printed or typewritten notice containing the information required by paragraph (1) of subdivision (a) of Section 1962 shall be placed in at least two conspicuous places.

(3) In the case of a single unit dwelling structure, the information to be disclosed under this section may be disclosed by complying with either paragraph (1) or (2).

(b) Except as provided in subdivision (a), all the provisions of Section 1962 shall be applicable.

Civil Code Section 1962.7: Service of Process on Noncomplying Owner

In the event an owner, successor owner, manager, or agent specified in Section 1961 fails to comply with the requirements of this chapter, service of process by a tenant with respect to a dispute arising out of the tenancy may be made by registered or certified mail sent to the address at which rent is paid, in which case the provisions of Section 1013 of the Code of Civil Procedure shall apply.

Appendix B

Sample Filled-In Forms

This appendix includes sample filled-in forms that should help you in completing your own forms. If you do not understand them, or are not sure if you have filled yours in correctly, you should ask the court clerk or consult an attorney. Most forms appear with the second page upside-down. California courts require this, and you should file the form like that. (*None of these forms are from the California Association of Realtors®.*)

The landlord will usually provide all the forms you will use. The forms contained in this book are the same or similar to those you will get from the landlord. They are included so you become more familiar with them when you get them from the landlord, making them easier to fill out.

The following sample forms are included in this appendix:

ATTORNEY OR PARTY WITHOUT ATTORNEY *(Name, state bar number, and address):*	FOR COURT USE ONLY
Louis Landlord 123 Home Circle Anytown, CA 90000 TELEPHONE NO.: (555)555-5555 FAX NO.: ATTORNEY FOR *(Name)*:	

INSERT NAME OF COURT, JUDICIAL DISTRICT, AND BRANCH COURT, IF ANY:
Municipal Court of California
100 Justice Way
Eviction City, CA 90001

CASE NAME:
Louis Landlord v. Thomas Tenant

CIVIL CASE COVER SHEET ☐ Limited ☐ Unlimited	**Complex Case Designation** ☐ Counter ☐ Joinder Filed with first appearance by defendant (Cal. Rules of Court, rule 1811)	CASE NUMBER: ASSIGNED JUDGE:

Please complete all five (5) items below.

1. Check **one** box below for the case type that best describes this case:

Auto Tort
- ☐ Auto (22)

Other PI/PD/WD (Personal Injury/Property Damage/Wrongful Death) Tort
- ☐ Asbestos (04)
- ☐ Product liability (24)
- ☐ Medical malpractice (45)
- ☐ Other PI/PD/WD (23)

Non-PI/PD/WD (Other) Tort
- ☐ Business tort/unfair business practice (07)
- ☐ Civil rights *(e.g., discrimination, false arrest)* (08)
- ☐ Defamation *(e.g., slander, libel)* (13)
- ☐ Fraud (16)
- ☐ Intellectual property (19)
- ☐ Professional negligence *(e.g., legal malpractice)* (25)
- ☐ Other non-PI/PD/WD tort (35)

Employment
- ☐ Wrongful termination (36)

- ☐ Other employment (15)

Contract
- ☒ Breach of contract/warranty (06)
- ☐ Collections *(e.g., money owed, open book accounts)* (09)
- ☐ Insurance coverage (18)
- ☐ Other contract (37)

Real Property
- ☐ Eminent domain/Inverse condemnation (14)
- ☐ Wrongful eviction (33)
- ☐ Other real property *(e.g., quiet title)* (26)

Unlawful Detainer
- ☐ Commercial (31)
- ☐ Residential (32)
- ☐ Drugs (38)

Judicial Review
- ☐ Asset forfeiture (05)
- ☐ Petition re: arbitration award (11)

- ☐ Writ of mandate (02)
- ☐ Other judicial review (39)

Provisionally Complex Civil Litigation (Cal. Rules of Court, rules 1800–1812)
- ☐ Antitrust/Trade regulation (03)
- ☐ Construction defect (10)
- ☐ Claims involving mass tort (40)
- ☐ Securities litigation (28)
- ☐ Toxic tort/Environmental (30)
- ☐ Insurance coverage claims arising from the above listed provisionally complex case types (41)

Enforcement of Judgment
- ☐ Enforcement of judgment *(e.g., sister state foreign, out-of-county abstracts)* (20)

Miscellaneous Civil Complaint
- ☐ RICO (27)
- ☐ Other complaint *(not specified above)* (42)

Miscellaneous Civil Petition
- ☐ Partnership and corporate governance (21
- ☐ Other petition *(not specified above)* (43)

2. This case ☐ is ☒ is not complex under rule 1800 of the California Rules of Court. If case is complex, mark the facto requiring exceptional judicial management:
   a. ☐ Large number of separately represented parties
   b. ☐ Extensive motion practice raising difficult or novel issues that will be time-consuming to resolve
   c. ☐ Substantial amount of documentary evidence
   d. ☐ Large number of witnesses
   e. ☐ Coordination and related actions pending in one or more co in other counties, states or countries, or in a federal court
   f. ☐ Substantial post-disposition judicial disposition

3. Type of remedies sought *(check all that apply)*:
   a. ☒ monetary   b. ☐ nonmonetary; declaratory or injunctive relief   c. ☐ punitive

4. Number of causes of action *(specify)*:

5. This case ☐ is ☒ is not a class action suit.

Date: June 1, 2002

Louis Landlord   ▶ *Louis Landlord*
. . . .
(TYPE OR PRINT NAME)   (SIGNATURE OF PARTY OR ATTORNEY FOR PARTY)

NOTICE
- Plaintiff must file this cover sheet with the first paper filed in the action or proceeding (except small claims cases or cases filed under the Probate, Family, or Welfare and Institutions Code). (Cal. Rules of Court, rule 982.2.)
- File this cover sheet in addition to any cover sheet required by local court rule.
- If this case is complex under rule 1800 et seq. of the California Rules of Court, you must serve a copy of this cover sheet on all other parties to the action or proceeding.
- Unless this is a complex case, this cover sheet shall be used for statistical purposes only.

Form Adopted for Mandatory Use
Judicial Council of California
982.2(b)(1) [Rev. January 1, 2000]

CIVIL CASE COVER SHEET

Cal. Rules of Court, rules 982.2, 1800–1
Standards of Judicial Administration,

131

This page intentionally left blank.

ATTORNEY OR PARTY WITHOUT ATTORNEY *(Name and Address)*:	TELEPHONE NO.:	FOR COURT USE ONLY
Louis Landlord 123 Home Circle Anytown, CA 90000	(555)555-5555	

ATTORNEY FOR *(Name)*:

NAME OF COURT: Municipal Court of California
STREET ADDRESS: 100 Justice Way
MAILING ADDRESS: Eviction City, CA 90000
CITY AND ZIP CODE:
BRANCH NAME: Eviction City Branch

PLAINTIFF: Louis Landlord

DEFENDANT: Thomas Tenant

[x] DOES 1 TO 10

COMPLAINT—Unlawful Detainer*

CASE NUMBER:

1. a. Plaintiff is (1) [x] an individual over the age of 18 years (4) [ ] a partnership
   (2) [ ] a public agency (5) [ ] a corporation
   (3) [ ] other *(specify)*:

   b. [ ] Plaintiff has complied with the fictitious business name laws and is doing business under the fictitious name of *(specify)*:

2. Defendants named above are in possession of the premises located at *(street address, apt. No., city, and county)*:
   100 Renter Circle, Apt. 9
   Eviction City, CA 90000

3. Plaintiff's interest in the premises is [x] as owner [ ] other *(specify)*:

4. The true names and capacities of defendants sued as Does are unknown to plaintiff.

5. a. On or about *(date)*: 2/1/98 defendants *(names)*: Thomas Tenant

   (1) agreed to rent the premises for a [x] month-to-month tenancy [ ] other tenancy *(specify)*:
   (2) agreed to pay rent of $ $900.00 payable [x] monthly [ ] other *(specify frequency)*:
   The rent is due on the [x] first of the month [ ] other day *(specify)*:

   b. This [x] written [ ] oral agreement was made with
   (1) [x] plaintiff (3) [ ] plaintiff's predecessor in interest
   (2) [ ] plaintiff's agent (4) [ ] other *(specify)*:

   c. [x] The defendants not named in item 5a are
   (1) [ ] subtenants (2) [ ] assignees (3) [x] other *(specify)*:

   d. [ ] The agreement was later changed as follows *(specify)*:

   e. [x] A copy of the written agreement is attached and labeled Exhibit 1.

6. [x] a. Defendants *(names)*: Thomas Tenant
   were served the following notice on the same date and in the same manner:
   (1) [x] 3-day notice to pay rent or quit (4) [ ] 3-day notice to quit
   (2) [ ] 3-day notice to perform covenants or quit (5) [ ] 30-day notice to quit
   (3) [x] other *(specify)*: Prejudgment Claim of Right to Possession

   b. (1) On *(date)*: May 14, 2002 the period stated in the notice expired at the end of the day.
   (2) Defendants failed to comply with the requirements of the notice by that date.

   c. All facts stated in the notice are true.

   d. [ ] The notice included an election of forfeiture.

   e. [x] A copy of the notice is attached and labeled Exhibit 2.

   f. [ ] One or more defendants was served (1) with a different notice, or (2) on a different date, or (3) in a different manner, as stated in attachment 6f. *(Check item 7c and attach a statement providing the information required by items 6a-e and 7 for each defendant.)*

NOTE: Do not use this form for evictions after sale (Code Civ. Proc., § 1161a).

(Continued on reverse)

Form Approved by the
Judicial Council of California
982.1(90) [Rev. July 1, 1996]

COMPLAINT—Unlawful Detainer

Civil Code, § 1940 et seq.;
Code of Civil Procedure, § 425.12

7. a. [X] The notice in item 6a was served on the defendants named in item 6a as follows:

    (1) [X] by personally handing a copy to defendant on (date): 5/10/02

    (2) [ ] by leaving a copy with (name or description):
           , a person of suitable age and discretion, on (date):   at defendant's [ ] residence [ ] business
           AND mailing a copy to defendant at defendant's place of residence on (date):
           because defendant cannot be found at defendant's residence or usual place of business.

    (3) [ ] by posting a copy on the premises on (date):   ([ ] and giving a copy to a person found residing at the premises) AND mailing a copy to defendant at the premises on (date):
        (a) [ ] because defendant's residence and usual place of business cannot be ascertained OR
        (b) [ ] because no person of suitable age or discretion can be found there.

    (4) [ ] (not for 3-day notice; see Civil Code section 1946 before using) by sending a copy by certified or registered mail addressed to defendant on (date):

    (5) [ ] (not for residential tenancies; see Civil Code section 1953 before using) in the manner specified in a written commercial lease between the parties.

  b. [X] (Name):   was served on behalf of all defendants who signed a joint written rental agreement.

  c. [ ] Information about service of notice on the defendants named in item 6f is stated in attachment 7c.

8. [ ] Plaintiff demands possession from each defendant because of expiration of a fixed-term lease.

9. [X] At the time the 3-day notice to pay rent or quit was served, the amount of **rent due** was $ 900

10. [X] The fair rental value of the premises is $ 30   per day.

11. [ ] Defendants' continued possession is malicious, and plaintiff is entitled to statutory damages under Code of Civil Procedure section 1174(b). (State specific facts supporting a claim up to $600 in attachment 11.)

12. [ ] A written agreement between the parties provides for attorney fees.

13. [ ] Defendants' tenancy is subject to the local rent control or eviction control ordinance of (city or county, title of ordinance, and date of passage):

    Plaintiff has met all applicable requirements of the ordinances.

14. [ ] Other allegations are stated in attachment 14.

15. Plaintiff remits to the jurisdictional limit, if any, of the court.

16. PLAINTIFF REQUESTS

  a. possession of the premises.
  b. costs incurred in this proceeding.
  c. [X] past due rent of $ 900
  d. [ ] reasonable attorney fees.
  e. [X] forfeiture of the agreement.

  f. [X] damages at the rate stated in item 10 from (date): June 1, 2002   for each day defendants remain in possession through entry of judgment.
  g. [ ] statutory damages up to $600 for the conduct alleged in item 11.
  h. [ ] other (specify):

17. [X] Number of pages attached (specify): 5

UNLAWFUL DETAINER ASSISTANT (Business and Professions Code sections 6400-6415)

18. (must be answered in all cases) An unlawful detainer assistant [X] did **not** [ ] did for compensation give advice or assistance with this form. (If plaintiff has received **any** help or advice for pay from an unlawful detainer assistant, state):

  a. Assistant's name:
  b. Telephone No.:
  c. Street address, city, and ZIP:

  d. County of registration: e. Registration No.:   f. Expires on (date):

Louis Landlord   ► *Louis Landlord*
(TYPE OR PRINT NAME)   (SIGNATURE OF PLAINTIFF OR ATTORNEY)

VERIFICATION

(Use a different verification form if the verification is by an attorney or for a corporation or partnership.)

I am the plaintiff in this proceeding and have read this complaint. I declare under penalty of perjury under the laws of the State of California that the foregoing is true and correct.

Date: June 1, 2003

Louis Landlord   ► *Louis Landlord*
(TYPE OR PRINT NAME)   (SIGNATURE OF PLAINTIFF)

SUMMONS
(CITACION JUDICIAL)

UNLAWFUL DETAINER—EVICTION
(PROCESO DE DESAHUCIO—EVICCION)

NOTICE TO DEFENDANT: *(Aviso a acusado)*

Thomas Tenant

YOU ARE BEING SUED BY PLAINTIFF:
(A Ud. le está demandando)

Louis Landlord

FOR COURT USE ONLY
(SOLO PARA USO DE LA CORTE)

You have **5 DAYS** after this summons is served on you to file a typewritten response at this court. (To calculate the five days, count Saturday and Sunday, but do not count other court holidays.)	*Después de que le entreguen esta citación judicial usted tiene un plazo de **5 DIAS** para presentar una respuesta escrita a máquina en esta corte. (Para calcular los cinco días, cuente el sábado y el domingo, pero no cuente ningún otro día feriado observado por la corte.)*
A letter or phone call will not protect you. Your typewritten response must be in proper legal form if you want the court to hear your case.	*Una carta o una llamada telefónica no le ofrecerá protección; su respuesta escrita a máquina tiene que cumplir con las formalidades legales apropiadas si usted quiere que la corte escuche su caso.*
If you do not file your response on time, you may lose the case, you may be evicted, and your wages, money, and property may be taken without further warning from the court.	*Si usted no presenta su respuesta a tiempo, puede perder el caso, le pueden obligar a desalojar su casa, y le pueden quitar su salario, su dinero y otras cosas de su propiedad sin aviso adicional por parte de la corte.*
There are other legal requirements. You may want to call an attorney right away. If you do not know an attorney, you may call an attorney referral service or a legal aid office *(listed in the phone book)*.	*Existen otros requisitos legales. Puede que usted quiera llamar a un abogado inmediatamente. Si no conoce a un abogado, puede llamar a un servicio de referencia de abogados o a una oficina de ayuda legal (vea el directorio telefónico).*

The name and address of the court is: *(El nombre y dirección de la corte es)*

Municipal Court of California
100 Justice Way - Eviction City, CA 90000

CASE NUMBER: *(Número del caso)*

The name, address, and telephone number of plaintiff's attorney, or plaintiff without an attorney, is:
(El nombre, la dirección y el número de teléfono del abogado del demandante, o del demandante que no tiene abogado, es)

Louis Landlord
123 Home Circle
Anytown, CA 90000

(Must be answered in all cases) An **unlawful detainer assistant (B&P 6400-6415)** [X] did **not** [ ] did for compensation give advice or assistance with this form. *(If plaintiff has received **any** help or advice for pay from an unlawful detainer assistant, state)*:

a. Assistant's name:

b. Telephone No.:

c. Street address, city, and ZIP:

d. County of registration:

e. Registration No.:

f. Expires on *(date)*:

Date:
(Fecha)

Clerk, by _____, Deputy
(Actuario) *(Delegado)*

[SEAL]

NOTICE TO THE PERSON SERVED: You are served

1. [X] as an individual defendant.
2. [ ] as the person sued under the fictitious name of *(specify)*:
3. [ ] on behalf of *(specify)*:

under: [ ] CCP 416.10 (corporation)   [ ] CCP 416.60 (minor)
[ ] CCP 416.20 (defunct corporation)   [ ] CCP 416.70 (conservatee)
[ ] CCP 416.40 (association or partnership)   [ ] CCP 416.90 (individual)
[ ] other:

4. [ ] by personal delivery on *(date)*:
(See reverse for Proof of Service)

Form Adopted by Rule 982
Judicial Council of California
982(a)(11) [Rev. January 1, 1997]

SUMMONS—UNLAWFUL DETAINER

Code of Civil Procedure, §§ 412.20, 1167

PROOF OF SERVICE

1. At the time of service I was at least 18 years of age and not a party to this action, and **I served copies** of the *(specify documents)*:

   3 day notice and prejudgment claim of right to possession

2. a. Party served *(specify name of party as shown on the documents served)*:

   Thomas Tenant

   b. Person served: [x] party in item 2a [ ] other *(specify name and title or relationship to the party named in item 2a)*:

   c. Address:
   100 Renter Circle, Apt. 9
   Eviction City, CA 90000

3. I served the party named in item 2
   a. [x] **by personally delivering** the copies (1) on *(date)*: 5/10/02 (2) at *(time)*: 6:00 p.m.
   b. [ ] **by leaving** the copies with or in the presence of *(name and title or relationship to person indicated in item 2b)*:

   (1) [ ] **(business)** a person at least 18 years of age apparently in charge at the office or usual place of business of the person served. I informed him or her of the general nature of the papers.
   (2) [ ] **(home)** a competent member of the household (at least 18 years of age) at the dwelling house or usual place of abode of the person served. I informed him or her of the general nature of the papers.
   (3) on *(date)*:   (4) at *(time)*:
   (5) [ ] A **declaration of diligence** is attached. *(Substituted service on natural person, minor, conservatee, or candidate.)*
   c. [ ] **by mailing** the copies to the person served, addressed as shown in item 2c, by first-class mail, postage prepaid,
   (1) on *(date)*:   (2) from *(city)*:
   (3) [ ] with two copies of the *Notice and Acknowledgment of Receipt* and a postage-paid return envelope addressed to me.
   (4) [ ] to an address outside California with return receipt requested. ← *(Attach completed form.)*
   d. [ ] **by causing** copies to be mailed. A declaration of mailing is attached.
   e. [ ] **other** *(specify other manner of service and authorizing code section)*:

4. The "Notice to the Person Served" (on the summons) was completed as follows:
   a. [x] as an individual defendant.
   b. [ ] as the person sued under the fictitious name of *(specify)*:
   c. [ ] on behalf of *(specify)*:
      under: [ ] CCP 416.10 (corporation)   [ ] CCP 416.60 (minor)   [ ] other:
             [ ] CCP 416.20 (defunct corporation)   [ ] CCP 416.70 (conservatee)
             [ ] CCP 416.40 (association or partnership) [ ] CCP 416.90 (individual)

5. **Person serving** *(name, address, and telephone number)*:

   Sally Server
   28 Main St.
   Eviction City, CA 90000
   (555)555-5555

   a. **Fee** for service: $
   b. [ ] Not a registered California process server
   c. [ ] Exempt from registration under B&P § 22350(b)
   d. [x] Registered California process server
      (1) [ ] Employee or independent contractor
      (2) Registration No.: 1234
      (3) County: Lemon
      (4) Expiration *(date)*: 6-2-03

6. [x] **I declare** under penalty of perjury under the laws of the State of California that the foregoing is true and correct.

7. [ ] **I am a California sheriff, marshal, or constable and** I certify that the foregoing is true and correct.

Date: June 1, 2003

▶ *Louis Landlord*

(SIGNATURE)

NOTICE: EVERYONE WHO LIVES IN THIS RENTAL UNIT MAY BE EVICTED BY COURT ORDER. READ THIS FORM IF YOU LIVE HERE AND IF YOUR NAME IS NOT ON THE ATTACHED SUMMONS AND COMPLAINT.

1. If you live here and you do not complete and submit this form within 10 days of the date of service shown on this form, you will be evicted without further hearing by the court along with the persons named in the Summons and Complaint.
2. If you file this form, your claim will be determined in the eviction action against the persons named in the Complaint.
3. If you do not file this form, you will be evicted without further hearing.

CLAIMANT OR CLAIMANT'S ATTORNEY (Name and Address):

TELEPHONE NO.:

Louis Landlord
123 Home Circle
Anytown, CA 90000

(555) 555-5555

FOR COURT USE ONLY

ATTORNEY FOR (Name):

NAME OF COURT: Municipal Court of California
STREET ADDRESS: 100 Justice Way
MAILING ADDRESS: Eviction City, CA 90000
CITY AND ZIP CODE:
BRANCH NAME: Eviction City Branch

PLAINTIFF: Louis Landlord

DEFENDANT: Thomas Tenant

PREJUDGMENT CLAIM OF RIGHT TO POSSESSION

CASE NUMBER: 1212

Complete this form only if ALL of these statements are true:
1. **You are NOT named in the accompanying Summons and Complaint.**
2. **You occupied the premises on or before the date the unlawful detainer (eviction) Complaint was filed.**
3. **You still occupy the premises.**

(To be completed by the process server)
DATE OF SERVICE:

(Date that this form is served or delivered, and posted, and mailed by the officer or process server)

I DECLARE THE FOLLOWING UNDER PENALTY OF PERJURY:

1. My name is (specify):

2. I reside at (street address, unit No., city and ZIP code):

3. The address of "the premises" subject to this claim is (address):

4. On (insert date): _____, the landlord or the landlord's authorized agent filed a complaint to recover possession of the premises. (This date is the court filing date on the accompanying Summons and Complaint.)

5. I occupied the premises on the date the complaint was filed (the date in item 4). I have continued to occupy the premises ever since.

6. I was at least 18 years of age on the date the complaint was filed (the date in item 4).

7. I claim a right to possession of the premises because I occupied the premises on the date the complaint was filed (the date in item 4).

8. I was not named in the Summons and Complaint.

9. I understand that if I make this claim of right to possession, I will be added as a defendant to the unlawful detainer (eviction) action.

10. (Filing fee) I understand that I must go to the court and pay a filing fee of $ _____ or file with the court the form "Application for Waiver of Court Fees and Costs." I understand that if I don't pay the filing fee or file with the court the form for waiver of court fees within 10 days from the date of service on this form (excluding court holidays), I will not be entitled to make a claim of right to possession.

(Continued on reverse)

CP10.5 [New January 1, 1991]

PREJUDGMENT CLAIM OF RIGHT TO POSSESSION

Code of Civil Procedure §§ 415.46, 715.010, 715.020, 1174.25

PLAINTIFF (Name): Louis Landlord	CASE NUMBER:
DEFENDANT (Name): Thomas Tenant	

NOTICE: If you fail to file this claim, you will be evicted without further hearing.

11. *(Response required within five days after you file this form.)* I understand that I will have *five days* (excluding court holidays) to file a response to the Summons and Complaint after I file this Prejudgment Claim of Right to Possession form.

12. **Rental agreement.** I have *(check all that apply to you)*:

   a. ☐ an oral rental agreement with the landlord.
   b. ☐ a written rental agreement with the landlord.
   c. ☐ an oral rental agreement with a person other than the landlord.
   d. ☐ a written rental agreement with a person other than the landlord.
   e. ☐ other *(explain)*:

I declare under penalty of perjury under the laws of the State of California that the foregoing is true and correct.

WARNING: Perjury is a felony punishable by imprisonment in the state prison.

Date: June 1, 2003

Louis Landlord
(TYPE OR PRINT NAME)

▶ *Louis Landlord*

(SIGNATURE OF CLAIMANT)

NOTICE: If you file this claim of right to possession, the unlawful detainer (eviction) action against you will be determined at trial. At trial, you may be found liable for rent, costs, and, in some cases, treble damages.

— **NOTICE TO OCCUPANTS** —

YOU MUST ACT AT ONCE if all the following are true:

1. You are NOT named in the accompanying Summons and Complaint.
2. You occupied the premises on or before the date the unlawful detainer (eviction) complaint was filed. *(The date is the court filing date on the accompanying Summons and Complaint.)*
3. You still occupy the premises.

(Where to file this form.) You can complete and SUBMIT THIS CLAIM FORM WITHIN 10 DAYS from the date of service (on the reverse of this form) at the court where the unlawful detainer (eviction) complaint was filed.

(What will happen if you do not file this form.) If you do not complete and submit this form and pay a filing fee or file the form for proceeding in forma pauperis if you cannot pay the fee), YOU WILL BE EVICTED.

After this form is properly filed, you will be added as a defendant in the unlawful detainer (eviction) action and your right to occupy the premises will be decided by the court. If you do not file this claim, you will be evicted without a hearing.

Appendix C

Blank Forms

The following forms are described in the text or should be self-explanatory. If you do not understand any aspect of a form, you should seek advice from an attorney before using. Some forms appear with the second page upside-down. California courts require this, and you should file the form that way. Before you write on any form, it is best to make copies in case you make a mistake. These forms can be torn out for use.

(*None of these forms are from the California Association of Realtors®.*)

Remember, the landlord will usually provide all the forms you will use. The forms contained in this book are the same or similar to those you will get from the landlord. They are included to familiarize you with them so that they are more easily understood before you get them from the landlord and, therefore, easier to fill out.

NOTE: *Although this book is copyrighted, purchasers of the book are granted permission to copy the forms created by the author for their own personal use or use in their law practice.*

TENANT APPLICATION

Name: _____
          First   *Last*   *Middle*

Date of Birth _____ Soc.Sec. No. _____ Dr. Lic. No. _____

Name: _____
          First   *Last*   *Middle*

Date of Birth _____ Soc.Sec. No. _____ Dr. Lic. No. _____

Names of all other occupants (all adult occupants must sign the lease). Include ages of any minor children.

Names: _____   _____

        _____   _____

Name(s) of anyone who will stay with you more than one week.

1. _____   2. _____

Your present address _____ _____
                        street   *city*   *state*   *zip*   *how long?*

Reason for leaving? _____

Present landlord _____ phone: _____

Address _____

Second previous landlord _____ phone: _____

Address _____ how long? _____

Have you ever been evicted? _____

Employer _____ phone: _____

Address _____ how long? _____

Job title _____ Supervisor _____

Current gross monthly income (before deductions) $_____

Other incomes $_____ Sources _____

Checking account: _____
                   bank   *branch*   *account no.*

Savings account: _____
                  bank   *branch*   *account no.*

Major credit card _____

Credit reference _____ Acct. no. _____

Balance owed _____ Monthly payment _____

Number of vehicles to kept at rental property? _____

_____
    make   *model*   *year*   *license no.*

_____
    make   *model*   *year*   *license no.*

Any pet? _____ Describe _____

Waterbed(s) or water filled furniture? _____ Describe _____

Emergency contact _____ _____
               name   *phone*

_____
             address

The undersigned hereby attest(s) that the above information is true and authorize(s) verification of any and all information given, as well as authorizing the obtaining of a credit report.

Application fee $_____   Deposit $ _____

Property to be rented is _____ Unit. _____

The rental amount is $ _____ per month plus a security deposit of $ _____.

Signature(s) of applicant(s)

_____ Date _____

_____ Date _____

DENIAL OF APPLICATION TO RENT

Your application to rent the property located at _____

_____

has been denied based in whole or in part on information supplied by the following credit reporting companies:

Company Name: _____

Address: _____

Phone: _____

Company Name: _____

Address: _____

Phone: _____

Company Name: _____

Address: _____

Phone: _____

You have the right to obtain a free copy of this report by contacting, within 60 days, the credit reporting agency indicated above and from any other consumer credit reporting agency that compiles and maintains files on a national basis.

You have the right to dispute the accuracy and completeness of any information in a consumer credit report furnished by a consumer credit reporting agency.

Date: _____

This page intentionally left blank.

INSPECTION REPORT

Date: _____

Unit: _____

AREA	CONDITION			
	Move-In		Move-Out	
	Good	Poor	Good	Poor
Yard/garden				
Driveway				
Patio/porch				
Exterior				
Entry light/bell				
Living room/Dining room/Halls:				
Floors/carpets				
Walls/ceiling				
Doors/locks				
Fixtures/lights				
Outlets/switches				
Other				
Bedrooms:				
Floors/carpets				
Walls/ceiling				
Doors/locks				
Fixtures/lights				
Outlets/switches				
Other				
Bathrooms:				
Faucets				
Toilet				
Sink/tub				
Floors/carpets				
Walls/ceiling				
Doors/locks				
Fixtures/lights				
Outlets/switches				
Other				
Kitchen:				
Refrigerator				
Range				
Oven				
Dishwasher				
Sink/disposal				
Cabinets/counters				
Floors/carpets				
Walls/ceiling				
Doors/locks				
Fixtures/lights				
Outlets/switches				
Other				
Misc.				
Closets/pantry				
Garage				
Keys				
Other				

This page intentionally left blank.

PET AGREEMENT

THIS AGREEMENT is made pursuant to that certain Lease dated _____ between _____ as Landlord and _____as Tenant, for rental of the property located at _____.

In consideration of $_____ as non-refundable cleaning payment and $_____ as additional security deposit paid by Tenant to Landlord, Tenant is allowed to keep the following pet(s): _____ on the premises _____ under the following conditions:

1. ❏ If the pet is a dog or cat, it is spayed or neutered.

    ❏ In the event the pet produces a litter, Tenant may keep them at the premises no longer than one month past weaning.

2. Tenant shall not engage in any commercial pet-raising activities.

3. No pets other than those listed above shall be kept on the premises without the further written permission of the Landlord.

4. Tenant agrees at all times to keep the pet from becoming a nuisance to neighbors and/or other tenants. This includes controlling the barking of the pet, if necessary and cleaning any animal waste on and about the premises.

5. In the event the pet causes destruction of the property, becomes a nuisance, or Tenant otherwise violates this agreement, Landlord may terminate the Lease according to California law.

6. An additional security deposit of $_____ shall be deposited with Landlord.

Date: _____

Landlord: Tenant:

_____   _____

_____   _____

This page intentionally left blank.

AGREEMENT FOR USE OF WATERBED

The property received a valid Certificate of Occupancy after January 1, 1973, and water filled furniture (herein called bedding) is permitted as provided by California Civil Code 1940.5

Landlord and Tenant agree as follows:

1.   Tenant shall provide owner with a valid waterbed insurance policy or certificate or insurance for property damage in the amount of $_____ (not less than $100,000) prior to installation of the bedding. The policy shall remain in effect until the bedding is permanently removed from the rental property.

2.   The bedding must have been constructed after January 1, 1973, and must conform to the rules and regulations of the Bureau of Home Furnishings pursuant to Section 19155 of the Business and Professional Code and shall display a label declaring said compliance.

3.   The bedding must not exceed the pounds-per-square-foot limitation of the rental property.

4.   Tenant shall give Landlord at least 24 hours written notice of installation, moving, or removal of the bedding and Landlord may be present at these times.

5.   Landlord may increase the security deposit by an additional one-half month's rent.

6.   All other provisions of Civil Code 1940.5 are incorporated into this agreement

_____   _____
Landlord/Agent   Date

_____   _____
Tenant   Date

_____   _____
Tenant   Date

This page intentionally left blank.

LEASE

LANDLORD:_____   TENANT:_____

_____   _____

PROPERTY:_____

IN CONSIDERATION of the mutual covenants and agreements herein contained, Landlord hereby leases to Tenant and Tenant hereby leases from Landlord the above-described property under the following terms:

    1. TERM. This lease shall be for a term of _____ beginning _____, _____ and ending _____, _____.

    2. RENT. The rent shall be $_____ per month and shall be due on or before the _____ day of each month. If rent is received more than three days late, a late charge of $_____ shall be paid.

    3. PAYMENT. Payment must be received by Landlord on or before the due date at the following address: _____ or such place as designated by Landlord in writing. Tenant understands that this may require early mailing. If a check bounces, Tenant agrees to pay a late charge of $_____, and Landlord may require future payments in cash, money order, or certified funds. Tenant is hereby notified that default of financial obligations under this agreement may be reported to credit reporting companies and may result in derogatory information on Tenant's credit report.

    4. DEFAULT. In the event Tenant defaults under any terms of this agreement, Landlord may recover possession as provided by Law and seek monetary damages.

    5. SECURITY. Landlord acknowledges receipt of the sum of $_____ as security deposit. This deposit may not be used as last month's rent. Landlord may withhold from the security deposit amounts necessary to cover unpaid rent, damages to the premises caused by the Tenant beyond ordinary wear and tear and cleaning of the premises, if necessary.

    Within three weeks after Landlord retakes possession of the premises, Landlord shall furnish Tenant with a written statement itemizing the amounts withheld with explanation and returning any unused portion of the deposit to Tenant.

    6. UTILITIES. Tenant agrees to pay all utility charges on the property except: _____ _____.

    7. MAINTENANCE. Tenant has examined the premises and has found them to be clean, safe, and in good repair and condition with the exception of the following:_____ _____

    Tenant agrees to return the premises to Landlord at the termination of the tenancy in the same clean, safe, good repair and condition, except for normal wear and tear.

    8. LOCKS. If Tenant adds or changes locks on the premises, Landlord shall be given copies of the keys. Landlord shall at all times have keys for access to the premises in case of emergencies.

    9. ASSIGNMENT AND SUBLETTING. Tenant may not sublet the premises nor any portion of the premises, nor may Tenant assign this agreement without written permission of Landlord.

    10. USE. Tenant shall not use the premises for any illegal purpose or any purpose which will increase the rate of insurance and shall not cause a nuisance for Landlord or neighbors. Tenant shall not create any environmental hazards on the premises.

    11. LAWN (CHECK AND INITIAL): Tenant agrees to maintain the lawn and other landscaping on the premises at Tenant's expense.   Yes _____   No _____   Initials _____

    12. LIABILITY. Tenant shall be responsible for insurance on his own property and agrees not to hold Landlord liable for any damages to Tenant's property on the premises.

    13. ACCESS. Landlord reserves the right to enter the premises in an emergency and also to inspect the premises as well as show the premises to prospective purchasers, tenants, and workers. Except in emergency, Landlord shall give Tenant at least 24 hours notice and shall enter only between 8am and 6pm, Monday through Saturday, except holidays.

    14. PETS. No pets shall be allowed on the premises except: _____.

    15. WATERBEDS: No waterbeds or liquid filled furniture shall be allowed on the premises without Landlord's written permission.

16. OCCUPANCY. The premises shall be occupied as a residence only, and shall be occupied only by the following persons. (List all occupants, both adults and minors) _____ _____.

17. TENANT'S APPLIANCES. Tenant agrees not to use any heaters, fixtures or appliances drawing excessive current without consent of the Landlord.

18. PARKING. Tenant agrees that no parking is allowed on the premises except: _____ _____. No boats, recreation vehicles or disassembled automobiles may be stored on the premises.

19. FURNISHINGS. Any articles provided to tenant and listed on attached schedule are to be returned in good condition at the termination of this agreement.

20. ALTERATIONS AND IMPROVEMENTS. Tenant shall make no alterations to the property without the written consent of the Landlord and any such alterations or improvements shall become the property of the Landlord.

21. SMOKE DETECTORS. Tenant shall be responsible for keeping smoke detectors operational and for changing battery when needed.

22. LIENS. The estate of Landlord shall not be subject to any liens for improvements contracted by Tenant.

23. HARASSMENT. Tenant shall not do any acts to intentionally harass the Landlord or other tenants.

24. ATTORNEYS FEES. In the event of legal action, the prevailing party (shall) (shall not) recover reasonable attorney's fees in addition to any other recovery.

25. SEVERABILITY. In the event any section of this agreement shall be held to be invalid, all remaining provisions shall remain in full force and effect.

26. RECORDING. This agreement shall not be recorded in any public records.

27. WAIVER. Any failure by Landlord to exercise any rights under this agreement shall not constitute a waiver of Landlord's rights.

28. SUBORDINATION. Tenants interest in the premises shall be subordinate to any encumbrances now or hereafter placed on the premises, to any advances made under such encumbrances, and to any extensions or renewals thereof. Tenant agrees to sign any documents indicating such subordination which may be required by lenders.

29. ATTACHMENTS: The following attachments are incorporated and made a part of this agreement. (Tenant should initial) A. _____ B. _____ C. _____ D. _____

30. ENTIRE AGREEMENT. This rental agreement, including the above initialed attachments, constitutes the entire agreement between the parties and may not be modified except in writing signed by all parties.

31. OWNER OR MANAGER. The owner or manager for service of legal notices is: _____ _____.

WITNESS the hands and seals of the parties hereto as of this _____ day of _____, _____.

LANDLORD: TENANT:

_____   _____

_____   _____

CONDOMINIUM LEASE

LANDLORD:_____   TENANT:_____

_____   _____

PROPERTY:_____

IN CONSIDERATION of the mutual covenants and agreements herein contained, Landlord hereby leases to Tenant and Tenant hereby leases from Landlord the above-described property under the following terms:

1. TERM. This lease shall be for a term of _____ beginning _____, _____ and ending _____, _____.

2. RENT. The rent shall be $_____ per month and shall be due on or before the _____ day of each month. If rent is received more than three days late, a late charge of $_____ shall be paid.

3. PAYMENT. Payment must be received by Landlord on or before the due date at the following address: _____ or such place as designated by Landlord in writing. Tenant understands that this may require early mailing. If a check bounces, Tenant agrees to pay a late charge of $_____, and Landlord may require future payments in cash, money order, or certified funds. Tenant is hereby notified that default of financial obligations under this agreement may be reported to credit reporting companies and may result in derogatory information on Tenant's credit report.

4. DEFAULT. In the event Tenant defaults under any terms of this agreement, Landlord may recover possession as provided by Law and seek monetary damages.

5. SECURITY. Landlord acknowledges receipt of the sum of $_____ as security deposit. This deposit may not be used as last month's rent. Landlord may withhold from the security deposit amounts necessary to cover unpaid rent, damages to the premises caused by the Tenant beyond ordinary wear and tear and cleaning of the premises, if necessary. Within three weeks after Landlord retakes possession of the premises, Landlord shall furnish Tenant with a written statement itemizing the amounts withheld with explanation and returning any unused portion of the deposit to Tenant.

6. UTILITIES. Tenant agrees to pay all utility charges on the property except: _____
_____.

7. MAINTENANCE. Tenant has examined the premises and has found them to be clean, safe, and in good repair and condition with the exception of the following:_____
_____

Tenant agrees to return the premises to Landlord at the termination of the tenancy in the same clean, safe, good repair and condition, except for normal wear and tear.

8. LOCKS. If Tenant adds or changes locks on the premises, Landlord shall be given copies of the keys. Landlord shall at all times have keys for access to the premises in case of emergencies.

9. ASSIGNMENT AND SUBLETTING. Tenant may not sublet the premises nor any portion of the premises, nor may Tenant assign this agreement without written permission of Landlord.

10. COMMON INTEREST PROPERTY. Tenant acknowledges that the premises are subject to a Declaration of Covenants, Conditions and Restrictions and Association Rules and Regulations. Copies of these documents are attached to and made part of this agreement. Tenant agrees to comply with the requirements of these documents and to reimburse Landlord for any fines or charges levied against Landlord for Tenant's failure to comply with these requirements.

11. USE. Tenant shall not use the premises for any illegal purpose or any purpose which will increase the rate of insurance and shall not cause a nuisance for Landlord or neighbors. Tenant shall not create any environmental hazards on the premises.

12. LAWN (CHECK AND INITIAL): Tenant agrees to maintain the lawn and other landscaping on the premises at Tenant's expense.   Yes _____   No _____   Initials _____

13. LIABILITY. Tenant shall be responsible for insurance on his own property and agrees not to hold Landlord liable for any damages to Tenant's property on the premises.

14. ACCESS. Landlord reserves the right to enter the premises in an emergency and also to inspect the premises as well as show the premises to prospective purchasers, tenants, and workers. Except in emergency,

Landlord shall give Tenant at least 24 hours notice and shall enter only between 8am and 6pm, Monday through Saturday, except holidays.

15. PETS. No pets shall be allowed on the premises except: _____.

16. WATERBEDS: No waterbeds or liquid filled furniture shall be allowed on the premises without Landlord's written permission.

17. OCCUPANCY. The premises shall be occupied as a residence only, and shall be occupied only by the following persons. (List all occupants, both adults and minors) _____
_____.

18. TENANT'S APPLIANCES. Tenant agrees not to use any heaters, fixtures or appliances drawing excessive current without consent of the Landlord.

19. PARKING. Tenant agrees that no parking is allowed on the premises except: _____
_____. No boats, recreation vehicles or disassembled automobiles may be stored on the premises.

20. FURNISHINGS. Any articles provided to tenant and listed on attached schedule are to be returned in good condition at the termination of this agreement.

21. ALTERATIONS AND IMPROVEMENTS. Tenant shall make no alterations to the property without the written consent of the Landlord and any such alterations or improvements shall become the property of the Landlord.

22. SMOKE DETECTORS. Tenant shall be responsible for keeping smoke detectors operational and for changing battery when needed.

23. LIENS. The estate of Landlord shall not be subject to any liens for improvements contracted by Tenant.

24. HARASSMENT. Tenant shall not do any acts to intentionally harass the Landlord or other tenants.

25. ATTORNEYS FEES. In the event of legal action, the prevailing party (shall) (shall not) recover reasonable attorney's fees in addition to any other recovery.

26. SEVERABILITY. In the event any section of this agreement shall be held to be invalid, all remaining provisions shall remain in full force and effect.

27. RECORDING. This agreement shall not be recorded in any public records.

28. WAIVER. Any failure by Landlord to exercise any rights under this agreement shall not constitute a waiver of Landlord's rights.

29. SUBORDINATION. Tenants interest in the premises shall be subordinate to any encumbrances now or hereafter placed on the premises, to any advances made under such encumbrances, and to any extensions or renewals thereof. Tenant agrees to sign any documents indicating such subordination which may be required by lenders.

30. ATTACHMENTS: The following attachments are incorporated and made a part of this agreement. (Tenant should initial) A. _____ B. _____
C. _____ D. _____

32. ENTIRE AGREEMENT. This rental agreement, including the above initialed attachments, constitutes the entire agreement between the parties and may not be modified except in writing signed by all parties.

32. OWNER OR MANAGER. The owner or manager for service of legal notices is: _____
_____.

WITNESS the hands and seals of the parties hereto as of this _____ day of
_____, _____.

LANDLORD: TENANT:

_____   _____

_____   _____

Rental Agreement

LANDLORD:_____   TENANT:_____

_____   _____

PROPERTY:_____

IN CONSIDERATION of the mutual covenants and agreements herein contained, Landlord hereby rents to Tenant and Tenant hereby rents from Landlord the above-described property under the following terms:

1. TERM. This Rental Agreement shall be for a month-to-month tenancy. Unless prohibited by law, this agreement may be terminated by either party or modified by Landlord upon service of 30 days written notice.

2. RENT. The rent shall be $_____ per month and shall be due on or before the _____ day of each month. If rent is received more than three days late, a late charge of $_____ shall be paid.

3. PAYMENT. Payment must be received by Landlord on or before the due date at the following address: _____ or such place as designated by Landlord in writing. Tenant understands that this may require early mailing. If a check bounces, Tenant agrees to pay a late charge of $_____, and Landlord may require future payments in cash, money order, or certified funds. Tenant is hereby notified that default of financial obligations under this agreement may be reported to credit reporting companies and may result in derogatory information on Tenant's credit report.

4. DEFAULT. In the event Tenant defaults under any terms of this agreement, Landlord may recover possession as provided by Law and seek monetary damages.

5. SECURITY. Landlord acknowledges receipt of the sum of $_____ as security deposit. This deposit may not be used as last month's rent. Landlord may withhold from the security deposit amounts necessary to cover unpaid rent, damages to the premises caused by the Tenant beyond ordinary wear and tear and cleaning of the premises, if necessary

Within three weeks after Landlord retakes possession of the premises, Landlord shall furnish Tenant with a written statement itemizing the amounts withheld with explanation and returning any unused portion of the deposit to Tenant.

6. UTILITIES. Tenant agrees to pay all utility charges on the property except: _____
_____.

7. MAINTENANCE. Tenant has examined the premises and has found them to be clean, safe, and in good repair and condition with the exception of the following:_____
_____

Tenant agrees to return the premises to Landlord at the termination of the tenancy in the same clean, safe, good repair and condition, except for normal wear and tear.

8. LOCKS. If Tenant adds or changes locks on the premises, Landlord shall be given copies of the keys. Landlord shall at all times have keys for access to the premises in case of emergencies.

9. ASSIGNMENT AND SUBLETTING. Tenant may not sublet the premises nor any portion of the premises, nor may Tenant assign this agreement without written permission of Landlord.

10. USE. Tenant shall not use the premises for any illegal purpose or any purpose which will increase the rate of insurance and shall not cause a nuisance for Landlord or neighbors. Tenant shall not create any environmental hazards on the premises.

11. LAWN (CHECK AND INITIAL): Tenant agrees to maintain the lawn and other landscaping on the premises at Tenant's expense.   Yes _____   No _____   Initials _____

12. LIABILITY. Tenant shall be responsible for insurance on his own property and agrees not to hold Landlord liable for any damages to Tenant's property on the premises.

13. ACCESS. Landlord reserves the right to enter the premises in an emergency and also to inspect the premises as well as show the premises to prospective purchasers, tenants, and workers. Except in emergency, Landlord shall give Tenant at least 24 hours notice and shall enter only between 8am and 6pm, Monday through Saturday, except holidays.

14. PETS. No pets shall be allowed on the premises except: _____.

15. WATERBEDS: No waterbeds or liquid filled furniture shall be allowed on the premises without Landlord's written permission.

16. OCCUPANCY. The premises shall be occupied as a residence only, and shall be occupied only by the following persons. (List all occupants, both adults and minors) _____
_____.

17. TENANT'S APPLIANCES. Tenant agrees not to use any heaters, fixtures or appliances drawing excessive current without consent of the Landlord.

18. PARKING. Tenant agrees that no parking is allowed on the premises except: _____
_____. No boats, recreation vehicles or disassembled automobiles may be stored on the premises.

19. FURNISHINGS. Any articles provided to tenant and listed on attached schedule are to be returned in good condition at the termination of this agreement.

20. ALTERATIONS AND IMPROVEMENTS. Tenant shall make no alterations to the property without the written consent of the Landlord and any such alterations or improvements shall become the property of the Landlord.

21. SMOKE DETECTORS. Tenant shall be responsible for keeping smoke detectors operational and for changing battery when needed.

22. LIENS. The estate of Landlord shall not be subject to any liens for improvements contracted by Tenant.

23. HARASSMENT. Tenant shall not do any acts to intentionally harass the Landlord or other tenants.

24. ATTORNEYS FEES. In the event of legal action, the prevailing party (shall) (shall not) recover reasonable attorney's fees in addition to any other recovery.

25. SEVERABILITY. In the event any section of this agreement shall be held to be invalid, all remaining provisions shall remain in full force and effect.

26. RECORDING. This agreement shall not be recorded in any public records.

27. WAIVER. Any failure by Landlord to exercise any rights under this agreement shall not constitute a waiver of Landlord's rights.

28. SUBORDINATION. Tenants interest in the premises shall be subordinate to any encumbrances now or hereafter placed on the premises, to any advances made under such encumbrances, and to any extensions or renewals thereof. Tenant agrees to sign any documents indicating such subordination which may be required by lenders.

29. ATTACHMENTS: The following attachments are incorporated and made a part of this agreement. (Tenant should initial) A. _____B. _____
C. _____ D. _____

30. ENTIRE AGREEMENT. This rental agreement, including the above initialed attachments, constitutes the entire agreement between the parties and may not be modified except in writing signed by all parties.

31. OWNER OR MANAGER. The owner or manager for service of legal notices is: _____
_____.

WITNESS the hands and seals of the parties hereto as of this _____ day of _____, _____.

LANDLORD: TENANT:

_____   _____

_____   _____

CONDOMINIUM RENTAL AGREEMENT

LANDLORD:_____   TENANT:_____

_____   _____

PROPERTY:_____

IN CONSIDERATION of the mutual covenants and agreements herein contained, Landlord hereby rents to Tenant and Tenant hereby rents from Landlord the above-described property under the following terms:

1. TERM. This Rental Agreement shall be for a month-to-month tenancy. Unless prohibited by law, this agreement may be terminated by either party or modified by Landlord upon service of 30 days written notice.

2. RENT. The rent shall be $_____ per month and shall be due on or before the _____ day of each month. If rent is received more than three days late, a late charge of $_____ shall be paid.

3. PAYMENT. Payment must be received by Landlord on or before the due date at the following address: _____ or such place as designated by Landlord in writing. Tenant understands that this may require early mailing. If a check bounces, Tenant agrees to pay a late charge of $_____, and Landlord may require future payments in cash, money order, or certified funds. Tenant is hereby notified that default of financial obligations under this agreement may be reported to credit reporting companies and may result in derogatory information on Tenant's credit report.

4. DEFAULT. In the event Tenant defaults under any terms of this agreement, Landlord may recover possession as provided by Law and seek monetary damages.

5. SECURITY. Landlord acknowledges receipt of the sum of $_____ as security deposit. This deposit may not be used as last month's rent. Landlord may withhold from the security deposit amounts necessary to cover unpaid rent, damages to the premises caused by the Tenant beyond ordinary wear and tear and cleaning of the premises, if necessary. Within three weeks after Landlord retakes possession of the premises, Landlord shall furnish Tenant with a written statement itemizing the amounts withheld with explanation and returning any unused portion of the deposit to Tenant.

6. UTILITIES. Tenant agrees to pay all utility charges on the property except: _____
_____.

7. MAINTENANCE. Tenant has examined the premises and has found them to be clean, safe, and in good repair and condition with the exception of the following:_____
_____
Tenant agrees to return the premises to Landlord at the termination of the tenancy in the same clean, safe, good repair and condition, except for normal wear and tear.

8. LOCKS. If Tenant adds or changes locks on the premises, Landlord shall be given copies of the keys. Landlord shall at all times have keys for access to the premises in case of emergencies.

9. ASSIGNMENT AND SUBLETTING. Tenant may not sublet the premises nor any portion of the premises, nor may Tenant assign this agreement without written permission of Landlord.

10. COMMON INTEREST PROPERTY . Tenant acknowledges that the premises are subject to a Declaration of Covenants, Conditions and Restrictions and Association Rules and Regulations. Copies of these documents are attached to and made part of this agreement. Tenant agrees to comply with the requirements of these documents and to reimburse Landlord for any fines or charges levied against Landlord for Tenant's failure to comply with these requirements.

11. USE. Tenant shall not use the premises for any illegal purpose or any purpose which will increase the rate of insurance and shall not cause a nuisance for Landlord or neighbors. Tenant shall not create any environmental hazards on the premises.

12. LAWN (CHECK AND INITIAL): Tenant agrees to maintain the lawn and other landscaping on the premises at Tenant's expense.   Yes _____   No _____   Initials _____

13. LIABILITY. Tenant shall be responsible for insurance on his own property and agrees not to hold Landlord liable for any damages to Tenant's property on the premises.

14. ACCESS. Landlord reserves the right to enter the premises in an emergency and also to inspect the premises as well as show the premises to prospective purchasers, tenants, and workers. Except in emergency, Landlord shall give Tenant at least 24 hours notice and shall enter only between 8am and 6pm, Monday through Saturday, except holidays.

15. PETS. No pets shall be allowed on the premises except: _____.

16. WATERBEDS: No waterbeds or liquid filled furniture shall be allowed on the premises without Landlord's written permission.

17. OCCUPANCY. The premises shall be occupied as a residence only, and shall be occupied only by the following persons. (List all occupants, both adults and minors) _____
_____.

18. TENANT'S APPLIANCES. Tenant agrees not to use any heaters, fixtures or appliances drawing excessive current without consent of the Landlord.

19. PARKING. Tenant agrees that no parking is allowed on the premises except: _____
_____. No boats, recreation vehicles or disassembled automobiles may be stored on the premises.

20. FURNISHINGS. Any articles provided to tenant and listed on attached schedule are to be returned in good condition at the termination of this agreement.

21. ALTERATIONS AND IMPROVEMENTS. Tenant shall make no alterations to the property without the written consent of the Landlord and any such alterations or improvements shall become the property of the Landlord.

22. SMOKE DETECTORS. Tenant shall be responsible for keeping smoke detectors operational and for changing battery when needed.

23. LIENS. The estate of Landlord shall not be subject to any liens for improvements contracted by Tenant.

24. HARASSMENT. Tenant shall not do any acts to intentionally harass the Landlord or other tenants.

25. ATTORNEYS FEES. In the event of legal action, the prevailing party (shall) (shall not) recover reasonable attorney's fees in addition to any other recovery.

26. SEVERABILITY. In the event any section of this agreement shall be held to be invalid, all remaining provisions shall remain in full force and effect.

27. RECORDING. This agreement shall not be recorded in any public records.

28. WAIVER. Any failure by Landlord to exercise any rights under this agreement shall not constitute a waiver of Landlord's rights.

29. SUBORDINATION. Tenants interest in the premises shall be subordinate to any encumbrances now or hereafter placed on the premises, to any advances made under such encumbrances, and to any extensions or renewals thereof. Tenant agrees to sign any documents indicating such subordination which may be required by lenders.

30. ATTACHMENTS: The following attachments are incorporated and made a part of this agreement. (Tenant should initial) A. _____ B. _____
C. _____ D. _____

31. ENTIRE AGREEMENT. This rental agreement, including the above initialed attachments, constitutes the entire agreement between the parties and may not be modified except in writing signed by all parties.

32. OWNER OR MANAGER. The owner or manager for service of legal notices is: _____
_____.

WITNESS the hands and seals of the parties hereto as of this _____ day of
_____, _____.

LANDLORD: TENANT:

_____   _____

_____   _____

AMENDMENT TO LEASE/RENTAL AGREEMENT

The undersigned parties to that certain agreement dated _____ ,
_____ on the premises known as _____ ,
hereby agree to amend said agreement as follows:

WITNESS the hands and seals of the parties hereto this ____ day of _____ ,
_____ .

Landlord: Tenant:

_____   _____

_____   _____

This page intentionally left blank.

GUARANTEE OF LEASE/RENTAL AGREEMENT

The undersigned Guarantor(s), in consideration of the Lease or Rental Agreement between _____ as Landlord and _____ as Tenant, dated _____, _____, and other good and valuable consideration, receipt whereof is hereby acknowledged, does/do hereby guaranty to Landlord, his/her/its successors and assigns, the faithful performance of the Lease or Rental Agreement and all sums due thereunder.

In the event of breach by Tenant of any of the terms of said Lease or Rental Agreement, including damage to the premises and attorney fees paid in enforcement of said agreement, Guarantor(s) shall be liable, and Landlord, his/her/its successors and assigns may have recourse against Guarantor(s) without first taking action against Tenant.

It is understood between the parties that this Guaranty does not confer any right to possession of the premises, or to require any notices to be served upon Guarantor(s), but only serves as an inducement for Landlord to enter into a Lease or rental Agreement with Tenant.

This Guaranty shall remain in effect until Tenant has fully complied with the Lease or Rental Agreement or until released in writing by landlord, his/her/its successors or assigns.

Date: _____, _____.

Guarantor(s):

_____

_____

This page intentionally left blank.

Disclosure of Information on Lead-Based Paint and/or Lead-Based Paint Hazards

Lead Warning Statement

Housing built before 1978 may contain lead-based paint. Lead from paint, paint chips, and dust can pose health hazards if not managed properly. Lead exposure is especially harmful to young children and pregnant women. Before renting pre-1978 housing, lessors must disclose the presence of known lead-based paint and/or lead-based paint hazards in the dwelling. Lessees must also receive a federally approved pamphlet on lead poisoning prevention.

Lessor's Disclosure

(a) Presence of lead-based paint and/or lead-based paint hazards (check (i) or (ii) below):

   (i) _____ Known lead-based paint and/or lead-based paint hazards are present in the housing (explain).

   _____

   _____

   (ii) _____ Lessor has no knowledge of lead-based paint and/or lead-based paint hazards in the housing.

(b) Records and reports available to the lessor (check (i) or (ii) below):

   (i) _____ Lessor has provided the lessee with all available records and reports pertaining to lead-based paint and/or lead-based paint hazards in the housing (list documents below).

   _____

   _____

   (ii) _____ Lessor has no reports or records pertaining to lead-based paint and/or lead-based paint hazards in the housing.

Lessee's Acknowledgment (initial)

(c) _____ Lessee has received copies of all information listed above.

(d) _____ Lessee has received the pamphlet *Protect Your Family from Lead in Your Home.*

Agent's Acknowledgment (initial)

(e) _____ Agent has informed the lessor of the lessor's obligations under 42 U.S.C. 4852(d) and is aware of his/her responsibility to ensure compliance.

Certification of Accuracy

The following parties have reviewed the information above and certify, to the best of their knowledge, that the information they have provided is true and accurate.

Lessor	Date	Lessor	Date
Lessee	Date	Lessee	Date
Agent	Date	Agent	Date

This page intentionally left blank.

CALIFORNIA LANDLORD DISCLOSURES

Date:

To:

    The undersigned owner(s) of the property located at _____

_____ make the following disclosures regarding

this property:

1. The property ❏ is ❏ is not within one mile of a former military base where ammunition

or explosives were kept.

2. ❏ Your electric bill only includes electricity used in your unit.

    ❏ You electric bill includes electricity used outside your unit as follows: _____

_____.

3. Other _____

_____

_____

_____

_____

_____

_____

_____

_____   _____
Owner   date   Owner   date

The undersigned tenant(s) acknowledge receipt and understanding of the above disclosures.

_____   _____
Tenant   date   Tenant   date

This page intentionally left blank.

INSPECTION REQUEST

Date:

To:

It will be necessary to enter your dwelling unit for the purpose of _____

_____

_____. If possible we would like

access on _____ at ____ o'clock ___.m.

In the event this is not convenient, please call to arrange another time.

Sincerely,

_____

Address:

Phone:

PROOF OF SERVICE

I, the undersigned, being at least 18 years of age, served this notice, of which this is a true copy, on
_____, the person(s) named above. The notice was served by:

❑   Personal delivery of a copy to the above named person(s).
❑   Delivery of a copy for each of the above named to a person of suitable age and discretion at the above named person(s) residence/business after attempting to personally serve the above named person(s) at his/her/their residence and place of business (if known) and mailing by first class mail a second copy to his/her/their residence.
❑   Posting a copy for each of the above named person(s) in a conspicuous place on the above identified property, being unable to personally serve a person of suitable age or discretion at the residence or known place(s) of business of the above named person(s) and mailing on the same date by first class mail a second copy to each above named person(s) to the address of the above identified property.

I declare under penalty of perjury that the above proof of service is true and correct.

Name _____   Date _____

This page intentionally left blank.

STATEMENT FOR REPAIRS

Date:

To:

It has been necessary to repair damage to the premises which you occupy which was caused by you or your guests. The costs for repairs were as follows:

This amount is your responsibility under the terms of the lease and California law and should be forwarded to us at the address below.

Sincerely,

_____

Address:

Phone:

PROOF OF SERVICE

I, the undersigned, being at least 18 years of age, served this notice, of which this is a true copy, on _____, the person(s) named above. The notice was served by:

❏   Personal delivery of a copy to the above named person(s).

❏   Delivery of a copy for each of the above named to a person of suitable age and discretion at the above named person(s) residence/business after attempting to personally serve the above named person(s) at his/her/their residence and place of business (if known) and mailing by first class mail a second copy to his/her/their residence.

❏   Posting a copy for each of the above named person(s) in a conspicuous place on the above identified property, being unable to personally serve a person of suitable age or discretion at the residence or known place(s) of business of the above named person(s) and mailing on the same date by first class mail a second copy to each above named person(s) to the address of the above identified property.

I declare under penalty of perjury that the above proof of service is true and correct.

Name _____   Date _____

This page intentionally left blank.

NOTICE OF CHANGE OF TERMS
CIVIL CODE SECTION 827

DATE:

To:

Dear

You are hereby notified that effective _____ the terms

of your rental agreement will be changed as follows:

❑　　Rent:　From $_____ per _____ To: $_____ per _____.

❑　　Other Changes:

Sincerely,

_____

Address:

Phone:

PROOF OF SERVICE

I, the undersigned, being at least 18 years of age, served this notice, of which this is a true copy, on
_____, the person(s) named above. The notice was served by:

❑　Personal delivery of a copy to the above named person(s).

❑　Delivery of a copy for each of the above named to a person of suitable age and discretion at the above named person(s) residence/business after attempting to personally serve the above named person(s) at his/her/their residence and place of business (if known) and mailing by first class mail a second copy to his/her/their residence.

❑　Posting a copy for each of the above named person(s) in a conspicuous place on the above identified property, being unable to personally serve a person of suitable age or discretion at the residence or known place(s) of business of the above named person(s) and mailing on the same date by first class mail a second copy to each above named person(s) to the address of the above identified property.

I declare under penalty of perjury that the above proof of service is true and correct.

Name _____　　　Date _____

This page intentionally left blank.

LETTER TO VACATING TENANT

DATE:

To:

Dear _____

    This letter is to remind you that your lease will expire on _____.
Please be advised that we do not intend to renew or extend the lease.

    The keys should be delivered to us at the address below on or before the end of the
lease along with your forwarding address. We will inspect the premises for damages, deduct
any amounts necessary for repairs and cleaning, and refund any remaining balance as
required by law.

                           Sincerely,

                 _____

                 Address:

                 Phone:

PROOF OF SERVICE

I, the undersigned, being at least 18 years of age, served this notice, of which this is a true copy, on
_____, the person(s) named above. The notice was served by:

- ❏   Personal delivery of a copy to the above named person(s).
- ❏   Delivery of a copy for each of the above named to a person of suitable age and discretion at the above named person(s) residence/business after attempting to personally serve the above named person(s) at his/her/their residence and place of business (if known) and mailing by first class mail a second copy to his/her/their residence.
- ❏   Posting a copy for each of the above named person(s) in a conspicuous place on the above identified property, being unable to personally serve a person of suitable age or discretion at the residence or known place(s) of business of the above named person(s) and mailing on the same date by first class mail a second copy to each above named person(s) to the address of the above identified property.

I declare under penalty of perjury that the above proof of service is true and correct.

Name _____   Date _____

This page intentionally left blank.

ANNUAL LETTER—CONTINUATION OF TENANCY

Date:

To:

Dear _____

    This letter is to remind you that your lease will expire on _____. Please advise us within _____ days as to whether you intend to renew your lease. If so, we will prepare a new lease for your signature(s).

    If you do not intend to renew your lease, the keys should be delivered to us at the address below on or before the end of the lease along with your forwarding address. We will inspect the premises for damages, deduct any amounts necessary for repairs and cleaning, and refund any remaining balance as required by law.

    If we have not heard from you as specified above we will assume that you will be vacating the premises and will arrange for a new tenant to move in at the end of your term.

                        Sincerely,

                     _____

                     Address:

                     Phone:

PROOF OF SERVICE

I, the undersigned, being at least 18 years of age, served this notice, of which this is a true copy, on _____, the person(s) named above. The notice was served by:

- ❏   Personal delivery of a copy to the above named person(s).
- ❏   Delivery of a copy for each of the above named to a person of suitable age and discretion at the above named person(s) residence/business after attempting to personally serve the above named person(s) at his/her/their residence and place of business (if known) and mailing by first class mail a second copy to his/her/their residence.
- ❏   Posting a copy for each of the above named person(s) in a conspicuous place on the above identified property, being unable to personally serve a person of suitable age or discretion at the residence or known place(s) of business of the above named person(s) and mailing on the same date by first class mail a second copy to each above named person(s) to the address of the above identified property.

I declare under penalty of perjury that the above proof of service is true and correct.

Name _____   Date _____

This page intentionally left blank.

NOTICE OF DISHONORED CHECK
AND DEMAND FOR PAYMENT

Date:

To:

You are advised that your check number _____, dated _____,

_____ in the amount of _____

dollars ($_____) was returned unpaid.

Unless this check is paid within thirty (30) days you may be liable for the amount of

the check plus triple the amount of the check in damages, but in no case less that one hun-

dred dollars ($100) or more than one thousand, five hundred dollars ($1,500).

Additionally, a report of your failure to pay this debt be made to a credit reporting

agency.

The applicable part of California Civil Code Section 1719 is as follows:

1719. (a) (1) Notwithstanding any penal sanctions that may apply, any person who passes a check on insufficient funds shall be liable to the payee for the amount of the check and a service charge payable to the payee for an amount not to exceed twenty-five dollars ($25) for the first check passed on insufficient funds and an amount not to exceed thirty-five dollars ($35) for each subsequent check to that payee passed on insufficient funds.

(2) Notwithstanding any penal sanctions that may apply, any person who passes a check on insufficient funds shall be liable to the payee for damages equal to treble the amount of the check if a written demand for payment is mailed by certified mail to the person who had passed a check on insufficient funds and the written demand informs this person of (A) the provisions of this section, (B) the amount of the check, and (C) the amount of the service charge payable to the payee. The person who had passed a check on insufficient funds shall have 30 days from the date the written demand was mailed to pay the amount of the check, the amount of the service charge payable to the payee, and the costs to mail the written demand for payment. If this person fails to pay in full the amount of the check, the service charge payable to the payee, and the costs to mail the written demand within this period, this person shall then be liable instead for the amount of the check, minus any partial payments made toward the amount of the check or service charge within 30 days of the written demand, and damages equal to treble that amount, which shall not be less than one hundred dollars ($100) nor more than one thousand five hundred dollars ($1,500). When a person becomes liable for treble damages for a check that is the subject of a written demand, that person shall no longer be liable for any service charge for that check and any costs to mail the written demand.

_____

Payee
Address:

Phone:

This page intentionally left blank.

ITEMIZED SECURITY DEPOSIT DISPOSITION
(CIVIL CODE SECTION 1950.5)

Date: _____

To: _____

_____

_____

Property Address: _____

Amount held as security: $_____
Interest: $_____
Total: $_____

DEDUCTIONS

1. Unpaid Rent: $_____ for (Dates) _____

_____

2. Repairs: $_____ for (Explanation) _____

_____

3. Cleaning: $_____ for (Explanation) _____

_____

4. Judgment: $_____ for (Explanation) _____

_____

Total Deductions: $_____
Amount owed by Tenant $_____
Amount owed to Tenant $_____

Further comments or explanations: _____

_____

_____

From: _____

_____

_____

Phone: _____

This page intentionally left blank.

THREE DAY NOTICE TO PAY RENT OR QUIT

To: _____
Tenants' and Subtenants' Full Names and Names of all Other Residents

_____
Address

_____
City, State, Zip Code

From: _____

Date: _____

You are hereby notified that you are indebted to me in the sum of $_____
(insert amount owed by Tenant)

for the rent from the following dates (do not go back more than one year):

$_____ for the period from _____ through _____

$_____ for the period from _____ through _____

$_____ for the period from _____ through _____

of the premises located at _____,
(insert address of leased premises, including county)

now occupied by you and that I demand payment of the rent or possession of the premises
within three days from the date of service of this notice, to-wit: on or before the _____ day
of _____, _____ (insert the date that is three days from the service of this
notice, excluding the date of service, Saturday, Sunday, and legal holidays).

_____
Signature

_____
Name of Landlord/Property manager
(Circle one)

_____
Address

_____
City, State, Zip Code

_____
Phone Number

Payment may be personally delivered to the above address between the hours of _____
AM/PM (circle one) and _____ AM/PM (circle one) on the following days of the week.
Mon. Tues. Wed. Thurs. Fri. Sat. Sun. (circle days for delivery).

Proof of Service

I, the undersigned, being at least 18 years of age, served this notice, of which this is a true copy, on _____, the person(s) named above. The notice was served by:

- ❏   Personal delivery of a copy to the above named person(s).
- ❏   Delivery of a copy for each of the above named to a person of suitable age and discretion at the above named person(s) residence/business after attempting to personally serve the above named person(s) at his/her/their residence and place of business (if known) and mailing by first class mail a second copy to his/her/their residence.
- ❏   Posting a copy for each of the above named person(s) in a conspicuous place on the above identified property, being unable to personally serve a person of suitable age or discretion at the residence or known place(s) of business of the above named person(s) and mailing on the same date by first class mail a second copy to each above named person(s) to the address of the above identified property.

I declare under penalty of perjury that the above proof of service is true and correct.

Name _____   Date _____

THREE DAY NOTICE TO COMPLY OR QUIT

To: _____

Tenant's Name

_____

Address

_____

City, State, Zip Code

From: _____

Date: _____

    You are hereby notified that you are not complying with your lease or rental agreement in that (insert noncompliance) _____ _____ _____. Demand is hereby made that you remedy the noncompliance within three days of service of this notice or your lease or rental agreement shall be deemed terminated and you shall vacate the premises upon such termination. Failure to vacate and surrender possession shall result in legal action to recover possession as well as damages and court costs.

_____

Landlord's Name_____

Address _____

_____

Phone Number _____

PROOF OF SERVICE

I, the undersigned, being at least 18 years of age, served this notice, of which this is a true copy, on _____, the person(s) named above. The notice was served by:

❏   Personal delivery of a copy to the above named person(s).

❏   Delivery of a copy for each of the above named to a person of suitable age and discretion at the above named person(s) residence/business after attempting to personally serve the above named person(s) at his/her/their residence and place of business (if known) and mailing by first class mail a second copy to his/her/their residence.

❏   Posting a copy for each of the above named person(s) in a conspicuous place on the above identified property, being unable to personally serve a person of suitable age or discretion at the residence or known place(s) of business of the above named person(s) and mailing on the same date by first class mail a second copy to each above named person(s) to the address of the above identified property.

I declare under penalty of perjury that the above proof of service is true and correct.

Name _____   Date _____

This page intentionally left blank.

THREE DAY NOTICE TO QUIT

(Tenant's Name and Address)

Dear _____:
        (Tenant's Name)

You are hereby notified that your lease is terminated immediately. You shall have three (3) days from delivery of this letter to vacate the premises. This action is taken because:

_____
Landlord's Name_____
Address _____
Phone Number _____

PROOF OF SERVICE

I, the undersigned, being at least 18 years of age, served this notice, of which this is a true copy, on _____, the person(s) named above. The notice was served by:

❏ Personal delivery of a copy to the above named person(s).

❏ Delivery of a copy for each of the above named to a person of suitable age and discretion at the above named person(s) residence/business after attempting to personally serve the above named person(s) at his/her/their residence and place of business (if known) and mailing by first class mail a second copy to his/her/their residence.

❏ Posting a copy for each of the above named person(s) in a conspicuous place on the above identified property, being unable to personally serve a person of suitable age or discretion at the residence or known place(s) of business of the above named person(s) and mailing on the same date by first class mail a second copy to each above named person(s) to the address of the above identified property.

I declare under penalty of perjury that the above proof of service is true and correct.

Name _____   Date _____

This page intentionally left blank.

30 Day Notice of Termination of Tenancy

To: _____
(Full names of tenants, subtenants, and all others in possession)

Rental Property: _____ Unit _____
(Street address, City, County, Zip)

You are notified that your tenancy of the above property is terminated effective 30 days from service of this notice or _____, whichever is later. At that time
(Date)
you must surrender possession of the premises. If you do not, an action for unlawful detainer will be filed. This may result in eviction as well as a judgment against you for payment of court costs.

You are obligated to continue to pay rent on the property until the date of termination.

_____
Date

_____
Landlord/Agent

Proof of Service

I, the undersigned, being at least 18 years of age, served this notice, of which this is a true copy, on _____, the person(s) named above. The notice was served by:

- ❏ Personal delivery of a copy to the above named person(s).
- ❏ Delivery of a copy for each of the above named to a person of suitable age and discretion at the above named person(s) residence/business after attempting to personally serve the above named person(s) at his/her/their residence and place of business (if known) and mailing by first class mail a second copy to his/her/their residence.
- ❏ Posting a copy for each of the above named person(s) in a conspicuous place on the above identified property, being unable to personally serve a person of suitable age or discretion at the residence or known place(s) of business of the above named person(s) and mailing on the same date by first class mail a second copy to each above named person(s) to the address of the above identified property.

I declare under penalty of perjury that the above proof of service is true and correct.

Name _____   Date _____

This page intentionally left blank.

NOTICE OF BELIEF OF ABANDONMENT
(REAL PROPERTY—CIVIL CODE SEC. 1951.3)

To: _____
(Full names of tenants, subtenants, and all others in possession)

Rental Property: _____ Unit _____
(Street address, City, County, Zip)

Pursuant to Civil Code Section 1951.3 you are notified that the rent on the above identified property rented by you has not been paid for 14 or more consecutive days and the Landlord believes that you have abandoned the property.

Pursuant to Civil Code Section 1951.2 the property will be deemed abandoned and your lease or rental agreement will terminate on _____, _____, which date is not less than 18 days after the mailing of this notice, unless prior to this date the undersigned receives written notice from you at the address below stating:

1. Your intent not to abandon the property and
2. An address where you may be served by certified mail for unlawful detainer of the property.

You are required to pay the rent due on this property as required by your lease or rental agreement and failure to do so may result in court action against you.

_____
Date

_____
Landlord/Agent

_____
Address

PROOF OF SERVICE

I, the undersigned, being at least 18 years of age, served this notice, of which this is a true copy, on _____, the person(s) named above. The notice was served by:

❑ Personal delivery of a copy to the above named person(s).
❑ Delivery of a copy for each of the above named to a person of suitable age and discretion at the above named person(s) residence/business after attempting to personally serve the above named person(s) at his/her/their residence and place of business (if known) and mailing by first class mail a second copy to his/her/their residence.
❑ Posting a copy for each of the above named person(s) in a conspicuous place on the above identified property, being unable to personally serve a person of suitable age or discretion at the residence or known place(s) of business of the above named person(s) and mailing on the same date by first class mail a second copy to each above named person(s) to the address of the above identified property.

I declare under penalty of perjury that the above proof of service is true and correct.

Name _____   Date _____

This page intentionally left blank.

ATTORNEY OR PARTY WITHOUT ATTORNEY *(Name, state bar number, and address)*:	FOR COURT USE ONLY

TELEPHONE NO.:   FAX NO.:

ATTORNEY FOR *(Name)*:

INSERT NAME OF COURT, JUDICIAL DISTRICT, AND BRANCH COURT, IF ANY:

CASE NAME:

CIVIL CASE COVER SHEET ☐ Limited ☐ Unlimited	**Complex Case Designation** ☐ Counter ☐ Joinder *Filed with first appearance by defendant* (Cal. Rules of Court, rule 1811)	CASE NUMBER: ASSIGNED JUDGE:

Please complete all five (5) items below.

1. Check **one** box below for the case type that best describes this case:

Auto Tort
- ☐ Auto (22)

Other PI/PD/WD (Personal Injury/Property Damage/Wrongful Death) Tort
- ☐ Asbestos (04)
- ☐ Product liability (24)
- ☐ Medical malpractice (45)
- ☐ Other PI/PD/WD (23)

Non-PI/PD/WD (Other) Tort
- ☐ Business tort/unfair business practice (07)
- ☐ Civil rights *(e.g., discrimination, false arrest)* (08)
- ☐ Defamation *(e.g., slander, libel)* (13)
- ☐ Fraud (16)
- ☐ Intellectual property (19)
- ☐ Professional negligence *(e.g., legal malpractice)* (25)
- ☐ Other non-PI/PD/WD tort (35)

Employment
- ☐ Wrongful termination (36)
- ☐ Other employment (15)

Contract
- ☐ Breach of contract/warranty (06)
- ☐ Collections *(e.g., money owed, open book accounts)* (09)
- ☐ Insurance coverage (18)
- ☐ Other contract (37)

Real Property
- ☐ Eminent domain/Inverse condemnation (14)
- ☐ Wrongful eviction (33)
- ☐ Other real property *(e.g., quiet title)* (26)

Unlawful Detainer
- ☐ Commercial (31)
- ☐ Residential (32)
- ☐ Drugs (38)

Judicial Review
- ☐ Asset forfeiture (05)
- ☐ Petition re: arbitration award (11)
- ☐ Writ of mandate (02)
- ☐ Other judicial review (39)

Provisionally Complex Civil Litigation (Cal. Rules of Court, rules 1800–1812)
- ☐ Antitrust/Trade regulation (03)
- ☐ Construction defect (10)
- ☐ Claims involving mass tort (40)
- ☐ Securities litigation (28)
- ☐ Toxic tort/Environmental (30)
- ☐ Insurance coverage claims arising from the above listed provisionally complex case types (41)

Enforcement of Judgment
- ☐ Enforcement of judgment *(e.g., sister state, foreign, out-of-county abstracts)* (20)

Miscellaneous Civil Complaint
- ☐ RICO (27)
- ☐ Other complaint *(not specified above)* (42)

Miscellaneous Civil Petition
- ☐ Partnership and corporate governance (21)
- ☐ Other petition *(not specified above)* (43)

2. This case ☐ is ☐ is not complex under rule 1800 of the California Rules of Court. If case is complex, mark the factors requiring exceptional judicial management:
   - a. ☐ Large number of separately represented parties
   - b. ☐ Extensive motion practice raising difficult or novel issues that will be time-consuming to resolve
   - c. ☐ Substantial amount of documentary evidence
   - d. ☐ Large number of witnesses
   - e. ☐ Coordination and related actions pending in one or more courts in other counties, states or countries, or in a federal court
   - f. ☐ Substantial post-disposition judicial disposition

3. Type of remedies sought *(check all that apply)*:
   - a. ☐ monetary   b. ☐ nonmonetary; declaratory or injunctive relief   c. ☐ punitive

4. Number of causes of action *(specify)*:

5. This case ☐ is ☐ is not a class action suit.

Date:

▶

....
(TYPE OR PRINT NAME)   (SIGNATURE OF PARTY OR ATTORNEY FOR PARTY)

NOTICE
- Plaintiff must file this cover sheet with the first paper filed in the action or proceeding (except small claims cases or cases filed under the Probate, Family, or Welfare and Institutions Code). (Cal. Rules of Court, rule 982.2.)
- File this cover sheet in addition to any cover sheet required by local court rule.
- If this case is complex under rule 1800 et seq. of the California Rules of Court, you must serve a copy of this cover sheet on all other parties to the action or proceeding.
- Unless this is a complex case, this cover sheet shall be used for statistical purposes only.

Form Adopted for Mandatory Use
Judicial Council of California
982.2(b)(1) [Rev. January 1, 2000]

CIVIL CASE COVER SHEET

Cal. Rules of Court, rules 982.2, 1800–1812;
Standards of Judicial Administration, § 19

This page intentionally left blank.

ATTORNEY OR PARTY WITHOUT ATTORNEY *(Name, state bar number, and address):*	FOR COURT USE ONLY
TELEPHONE NO.: FAX NO. *(Optional):* E-MAIL ADDRESS *(Optional):* ATTORNEY FOR *(Name):*	

SUPERIOR COURT OF CALIFORNIA, COUNTY OF
   STREET ADDRESS:
   MAILING ADDRESS:
   CITY AND ZIP CODE:
   BRANCH NAME:

PLAINTIFF:

DEFENDANT:

☐ DOES 1 TO _____

COMPLAINT—Unlawful Detainer* ☐ **COMPLAINT** ☐ **AMENDED COMPLAINT** *(Number):*	CASE NUMBER:

Jurisdiction *(check all that apply):*

☐ **ACTION IS A LIMITED CIVIL CASE**
   Amount Demanded   ☐   **does not exceed $10,000**
                         ☐   **exceeds $10,000, but does not exceed $25,000**
☐ **ACTION IS AN UNLIMITED CIVIL CASE (exceeds $25,000)**
☐ **ACTION IS RECLASSIFIED by this amended complaint or cross–complaint**
    ☐ **from limited to unlimited**
    ☐ **from unlimited to limited**

1. PLAINTIFF *(names):*

   alleges causes of action against DEFENDANT *(names):*

2. a. Plaintiff is   (1) ☐ an individual over the age of 18 years   (4) ☐ a partnership
                      (2) ☐ a public agency   (5) ☐ a corporation
                      (3) ☐ other *(specify):*
   b. ☐ Plaintiff has complied with the fictitious business name laws and is doing business under the fictitious name of
      (specify):

3. Defendants named above are in possession of the premises located at *(street address, apt. no., city, zip code, and county):*

4. Plaintiff's interest in the premises is   ☐ as owner   ☐ other *(specify):*

5. The true names and capacities of defendants sued as Does are unknown to plaintiff.

6. a. On or about *(date):*   defendants *(names):*

     (1) agreed to rent the premises for a   ☐ month-to-month tenancy   ☐ other tenancy *(specify):*
     (2) agreed to pay rent of $ payable ☐ monthly ☐ other *(specify frequency):*
        The rent is due on the   ☐ first of the month   ☐ other day *(specify):*
   b. This ☐ written ☐ oral agreement was made with
     (1) ☐ plaintiff   (3) ☐ plaintiff's predecessor in interest
     (2) ☐ plaintiff's agent   (4) ☐ other *(specify):*
   c. ☐ The defendants not named in item 6a are
     (1) ☐ subtenants   (2) ☐ assignees   (3) ☐ other *(specify):*
   d. ☐ The agreement was later changed as follows *(specify):*

   e. ☐ A copy of the written agreement is attached and labeled Exhibit 1.

*NOTE: Do not use this form for evictions after sale (Code Civ. Proc., § 1161a).

Form Approved for Optional Use
 Judicial Council of California
 982.1(90) [Rev. July 1, 2002]

COMPLAINT—Unlawful Detainer

Civil Code, § 1940 et seq.;
Code of Civil Procedure, § 425.12

PLAINTIFF (Name):	CASE NUMBER:
DEFENDANT (Name):	

7. a. [ ] Defendants (names):

were served the following notice on the same date and in the same manner:
(1) [ ] 3-day notice to pay rent or quit　　　(4) [ ] 3-day notice to quit
(2) [ ] 3-day notice to perform covenants or quit　　　(5) [ ] 30-day notice to quit
(3) [ ] other (specify):

b. (1) [ ] On (date): the period stated in the notice expired at the end of the day.
(2) Defendants failed to comply with the requirements of the notice by that date.

c. All facts stated in the notice are true.

d. [ ] The notice included an election of forfeiture.

e. [ ] A copy of the notice is attached and labeled Exhibit 2.

f. [ ] One or more defendants was served (1) with a different notice, or (2) on a different date, or (3) in a different manner, as stated in attachment 7f. (Check item 8c and attach a statement providing the information required by items 7a-e and 8 for each defendant.)

8. a. [ ] The notice in item 7a named on the defendants named in item 7a as follows:
(1) [ ] by personally handing a copy to defendant on (date):
(2) [ ] by leaving a copy with (name or description):
, a person
of suitable age and discretion, on (date): at defendant's [ ] residence [ ] business
AND mailing a copy to defendant at defendant's place of residence on (date):
because defendant cannot be found at defendant's residence or usual place of business.
(3) [ ] by posting a copy on the premises on (date): and giving a copy to a person found
residing at the premises) AND mailing a copy to defendant at the premises on (date):
(a) [ ] because defendant's residence and usual place of business cannot be ascertained OR
(b) [ ] because no person of suitable age or discretion can be found there.
(4) [ ] (not for 3-day notice; see Civil Code section 1946 before using) by sending a copy by certified or registered
mail addressed to defendant on (date):
(5) [ ] (not for residential tenancies; see Civil Code section 1953 before using) in the manner specified in a written
commercial lease between the parties.

b. [ ] (Name): was served on behalf of all defendants who signed a joint written rental agreement.

c. [ ] Information about service of notice on the defendants named in item 7f is stated in attachment 8c.

9. [ ] Plaintiff demands possession from each defendant because of expiration of a fixed-term lease.

10. [ ] At the time the 3-day notice to pay rent or quit was served, the amount of rent **due** was $

11. [ ] The fair rental value of the premises is $ per day.

12. [ ] Defendants' continued possession is malicious, and plaintiff is entitled to statutory damages under Code of Civil Procedure section 1174(b). (State specific facts supporting a claim up to $600 in attachment 12.)

13. [ ] A written agreement between the parties provides for attorney fees.

14. [ ] Defendants' tenancy is subject to the local rent control or eviction control ordinance of (city or county, title of ordinance, and date of passage):

Plaintiff has met all applicable requirements of the ordinances.

15. [ ] Other allegations are stated in attachment 15.

16. Plaintiff remits to the jurisdictional limit, if any, of the court.

17. PLAINTIFF REQUESTS
a. possession of the premises.
b. costs incurred in this proceeding.
c. [ ] past due rent of $
d. [ ] reasonable attorney fees.
e. [ ] forfeiture of the agreement.
f. [ ] damages at the rate stated in item 11 from
(date): for each day that
defendants remain in possession through entry of judgment.
g. [ ] statutory damages up to $600 for the conduct alleged in item 12.
h. [ ] other (specify):

18. [ ] Number of pages attached (specify):

PLAINTIFF (Name):	CASE NUMBER:
DEFENDANT (Name):	

UNLAWFUL DETAINER ASSISTANT (Business and Professions Code sections 6400-6415)

19. *This item must be answered in all cases.* An unlawful detainer assistant ☐ did **not** ☐ did for compensation give advice or assistance with this form. *(If plaintiff has received **any** help or advice for pay from an unlawful detainer assistant, state):*

   a. Assistant's name: b. Telephone No.:

   c. Street address, city, and ZIP:

   d. County of registration: e. Registration No.:   f. Expires on *(date):*

▶

_____   _____
(TYPE OR PRINT NAME)   (SIGNATURE OF PLAINTIFF OR ATTORNEY)

VERIFICATION

(Use a different verification form if the verification is by an attorney or for a corporation or partnership.)

I am the plaintiff in this proceeding and have read this complaint. I declare under penalty of perjury under the laws of the State of California that the foregoing is true and correct.

Date:

▶

_____   _____
(TYPE OR PRINT NAME)   (SIGNATURE OF PLAINTIFF)

This page intentionally left blank.

SUMMONS
(CITACION JUDICIAL)

UNLAWFUL DETAINER—EVICTION
(PROCESO DE DESAHUCIO—EVICCION)

NOTICE TO DEFENDANT: *(Aviso a acusado)*

FOR COURT USE ONLY
(SOLO PARA USO DE LA CORTE)

YOU ARE BEING SUED BY PLAINTIFF:
(A Ud. le está demandando)

You have **5 DAYS** after this summons is served on you to file a typewritten response at this court. (To calculate the five days, count Saturday and Sunday, but do not count other court holidays.)	*Después de que le entreguen esta citación judicial usted tiene un plazo de 5 DIAS para presentar una respuesta escrita a máquina en esta corte. (Para calcular los cinco días, cuente el sábado y el domingo, pero no cuente ningún otro día feriado observado por la corte.)*
A letter or phone call will not protect you. Your typewritten response must be in proper legal form if you want the court to hear your case.	*Una carta o una llamada telefónica no le ofrecerá protección; su respuesta escrita a máquina tiene que cumplir con las formalidades legales apropiadas si usted quiere que la corte escuche su caso.*
If you do not file your response on time, you may lose the case, and you may be evicted, and your wages, money, and property may be taken without further warning from the court.	*Si usted no presenta su respuesta a tiempo, puede perder el caso, le pueden obligar a desalojar su casa, y le pueden quitar su salario, su dinero y otras cosas de su propiedad sin aviso adicional por parte de la corte.*
There are other legal requirements. You may want to call an attorney right away. If you do not know an attorney, you may call an attorney referral service or a legal aid office *(listed in the phone book)*.	*Existen otros requisitos legales. Puede que usted quiera llamar a un abogado inmediatamente. Si no conoce a un abogado, puede llamar a un servicio de referencia de abogados o a una oficina de ayuda legal (vea el directorio telefónico).*

The name and address of the court is: *(El nombre y dirección de la corte es)*

CASE NUMBER: *(Número del caso)*

The name, address, and telephone number of plaintiff's attorney, or plaintiff without an attorney, is:
(El nombre, la dirección y el número de teléfono del abogado del demandante, o del demandante que no tiene abogado, es)

(Must be answered in all cases) An **unlawful detainer assistant (B&P 6400-6415)** ☐ did **not** ☐ did for compensation give advice or assistance with this form. *(If plaintiff has received any help or advice for pay from an unlawful detainer assistant, state)*:

a. Assistant's name:

b. Telephone No.:

c. Street address, city, and ZIP:

d. County of registration:

e. Registration No.:

f. Expires on *(date)*:

Date:
(Fecha)

Clerk, by _____ , Deputy
(Actuario) _____ *(Delegado)*

[SEAL]

NOTICE TO THE PERSON SERVED: You are served
1. ☐ as an individual defendant.
2. ☐ as the person sued under the fictitious name of *(specify)*:

3. ☐ on behalf of *(specify)*:

under: ☐ CCP 416.10 (corporation)   ☐ CCP 416.60 (minor)
☐ CCP 416.20 (defunct corporation)   ☐ CCP 416.70 (conservatee)
☐ CCP 416.40 (association or partnership)   ☐ CCP 416.90 (individual)
☐ other:
4. ☐ by personal delivery on *(date)*:
(See reverse for Proof of Service)

SUMMONS—UNLAWFUL DETAINER

Code of Civil Procedure, §§ 412.20, 1167

PLAINTIFF:	CASE NUMBER:
DEFENDANT:	

PROOF OF SERVICE

1. At the time of service I was at least 18 years of age and not a party to this action, and I **served copies** of the *(specify documents)*:

2. a. Party served *(specify name of party as shown on the documents served)*:

   b. Person served: ☐ party in item 2a ☐ other *(specify name and title or relationship to the party named in item 2a)*:

   c. Address:

3. I served the party named in item 2
   a. ☐ **by personally delivering** the copies (1) on *(date)*:   (2) at *(time)*:
   b. ☐ **by leaving** the copies with or in the presence of *(name and title or relationship to person indicated in item 2b)*:

   (1) ☐ **(business)** a person at least 18 years of age apparently in charge at the office or usual place of business of the person served. I informed him or her of the general nature of the papers.

   (2) ☐ **(home)** a competent member of the household (at least 18 years of age) at the dwelling house or usual place of abode of the person served. I informed him or her of the general nature of the papers.

   (3) on *(date)*:   (4) at *(time)*:

   (5) ☐ A **declaration of diligence** is attached. *(Substituted service on natural person, minor, conservatee, or candidate.)*

   c. ☐ **by mailing** the copies to the person served, addressed as shown in item 2c, by first-class mail, postage prepaid.

   (1) on *(date)*:   (2) from *(city)*:

   (3) ☐ with two copies of the *Notice and Acknowledgment of Receipt* and a postage-paid return envelope addressed to me.

   (4) ☐ to an address outside California with return receipt requested.   →   *(Attach completed form.)* ⌐

   d. ☐ **by causing** copies to be mailed. A declaration of mailing is attached.

   e. ☐ **other** *(specify other manner of service and authorizing code section)*:

4. The "Notice to the Person Served" (on the summons) was completed as follows:
   a. ☐ as an individual defendant.
   b. ☐ as the person sued under the fictitious name of *(specify)*:
   c. ☐ on behalf of *(specify)*:

   under: ☐ CCP 416.10 (corporation)   ☐ CCP 416.60 (minor)   ☐ other:
   ☐ CCP 416.20 (defunct corporation)   ☐ CCP 416.70 (conservatee)
   ☐ CCP 416.40 (association or partnership)   ☐ CCP 416.90 (individual)

5. **Person serving** *(name, address, and telephone number)*:   a. **Fee for service:** $
   b. ☐ Not a registered California process server
   c. ☐ Exempt from registration under B&P § 22350(b)
   d. ☐ Registered California process server
        (1) ☐ Employee or independent contractor
        (2) Registration No.:
        (3) County:
        (4) Expiration *(date)*:

6. ☐ I **declare** under penalty of perjury under the laws of the State of California that the foregoing is true and correct.

7. ☐ I am a **California sheriff, marshal, or constable and** I certify that the foregoing is true and correct.

Date: ▶

                          (SIGNATURE)

PROOF OF SERVICE
(Summons—Unlawful Detainer)

NOTICE: EVERYONE WHO LIVES IN THIS RENTAL UNIT MAY BE EVICTED BY COURT ORDER. READ THIS FORM IF YOU LIVE HERE AND IF YOUR NAME IS NOT ON THE ATTACHED SUMMONS AND COMPLAINT.

1. If you live here and you do not complete and submit this form within 10 days of the date of service shown on this form, you will be evicted without further hearing by the court along with the persons named in the Summons and Complaint.
2. If you file this form, your claim will be determined in the eviction action against the persons named in the Complaint.
3. If you do not file this form, you will be evicted without further hearing.

CLAIMANT OR CLAIMANT'S ATTORNEY *(Name and Address):*

TELEPHONE NO.:

FOR COURT USE ONLY

ATTORNEY FOR *(Name):*

NAME OF COURT:

STREET ADDRESS:

MAILING ADDRESS:

CITY AND ZIP CODE:

BRANCH NAME:

PLAINTIFF:

DEFENDANT:

PREJUDGMENT CLAIM OF RIGHT TO POSSESSION

CASE NUMBER:

Complete this form only if ALL of these statements are true:
1. **You are NOT named in the accompanying Summons and Complaint.**
2. **You occupied the premises on or before the date the unlawful detainer (eviction) Complaint was filed.**
3. **You still occupy the premises.**

(To be completed by the process server)
DATE OF SERVICE:

(Date that this form is served or delivered, and posted, and mailed by the officer or process server)

I DECLARE THE FOLLOWING UNDER PENALTY OF PERJURY:

1. My name is *(specify):*

2. I reside at *(street address, unit No., city and ZIP code):*

3. The address of "the premises" subject to this claim is *(address):*

4. On *(insert date):* _____, the landlord or the landlord's authorized agent filed a complaint to recover possession of the premises. *(This date is the court filing date on the accompanying Summons and Complaint.*

5. I occupied the premises on the date the complaint was filed *(the date in item 4).* I have continued to occupy the premises ever since.

6. I was at least 18 years of age on the date the complaint was filed *(the date in item 4).*

7. I claim a right to possession of the premises because I occupied the premises on the date the complaint was filed *(the date in item 4).*

8. I was not named in the Summons and Complaint.

9. I understand that if I make this claim of right to possession, I will be added as a defendant to the unlawful detainer (eviction) action.

10. *(Filing fee)* I understand that I must go to the court and pay a filing fee of $ _____ or file with the court the form "Application for Waiver of Court Fees and Costs." I understand that if I don't pay the filing fee or file with the court the form for waiver of court fees within 10 days from the date of service on this form (excluding court holidays), I will not be entitled to make a claim of right to possession.

(Continued on reverse)

CP10.5 [New January 1, 1991]

PREJUDGMENT CLAIM OF RIGHT TO POSSESSION

Code of Civil Procedure §§ 415.46, 715.010, 715.020, 1174.25

PLAINTIFF (Name):	CASE NUMBER:
DEFENDANT (Name):	

NOTICE: If you fail to file this claim, you will be evicted without further hearing.

11. *(Response required within five days after you file this form)* I understand that I will have five days (excluding court holidays) to file a response to the Summons and Complaint after I file this Prejudgment Claim of Right to Possession form.

12. **Rental agreement.** I have *(check all that apply to you)*:

   a. ☐ an oral rental agreement with the landlord.
   b. ☐ a written rental agreement with the landlord.
   c. ☐ an oral rental agreement with a person other than the landlord.
   d. ☐ a written rental agreement with a person other than the landlord.
   e. ☐ other *(explain)*:

I declare under penalty of perjury under the laws of the State of California that the foregoing is true and correct.

WARNING: Perjury is a felony punishable by imprisonment in the state prison.

Date:

▶

. . . .

(TYPE OR PRINT NAME)   (SIGNATURE OF CLAIMANT)

NOTICE: If you file this claim of right to possession, the unlawful detainer (eviction) action against you will be determined at trial. At trial, you may be found liable for rent, costs, and, in some cases, treble damages.

— NOTICE TO OCCUPANTS —

YOU MUST ACT AT ONCE if all the following are true:

1. **You are NOT named in the accompanying Summons and Complaint.**
2. **You occupied the premises on or before the date the unlawful detainer (eviction) complaint was filed.** *(The date is the court filing date on the accompanying Summons and Complaint.)*
3. **You still occupy the premises.**

(Where to file this form) You can complete and SUBMIT THIS CLAIM FORM WITHIN 10 DAYS from the date of service (on the reverse of this form) at the court where the unlawful detainer (eviction) complaint was filed.

(What will happen if you do not file this form) If you do not complete and submit this form and pay a filing fee or file the form for proceeding in forma pauperis if you cannot pay the fee), **YOU WILL BE EVICTED.**

After this form is properly filed, you will be added as a defendant in the unlawful detainer (eviction) action and your right to occupy the premises will be decided by the court. If you do not file this claim, you will be evicted without a hearing.

ATTORNEY OR PARTY WITHOUT ATTORNEY *(Name and Address)*:	TELEPHONE NO.:	**FOR COURT USE ONLY**

ATTORNEY FOR *(Name)*:

NAME OF COURT:

STREET ADDRESS:

MAILING ADDRESS:

CITY AND ZIP CODE:

BRANCH NAME:

PLAINTIFF:

DEFENDANT:

ANSWER—Unlawful Detainer	CASE NUMBER:

1. Defendant *(names)*:

answers the complaint as follows:

2. **Check ONLY ONE of the next two boxes:**
   a. ☐ Defendant generally denies each statement of the complaint. *(Do not check this box if the complaint demands more than $1,000).*
   b. ☐ Defendant admits that all of the statements of the complaint are true EXCEPT
      (1) Defendant claims the following statements of the complaint are false *(use paragraph numbers from the complaint or explain)*:

      ☐ Continued on Attachment 2b(1).
      (2) Defendant has no information or belief that the following statements of the complaint are true, so defendant denies them *(use paragraph numbers from the complaint or explain)*:

      ☐ Continued on Attachment 2b(2).

3. AFFIRMATIVE DEFENSES   (**NOTE:** *For each box checked, you must state brief facts to support it in the space provided at the top of page two (item 3j).)*
   a. ☐ *(nonpayment of rent only)* Plaintiff has breached the warranty to provide habitable premises.
   b. ☐ *(nonpayment of rent only)* Defendant made needed repairs and properly deducted the cost from the rent, and plaintiff did not give proper credit.
   c. ☐ *(nonpayment of rent only)* On *(date)*:   , before the notice to pay or quit expired, defendant offered the rent due but plaintiff would not accept it.
   d. ☐ Plaintiff waived, changed, or canceled the notice to quit.
   e. ☐ Plaintiff served defendant with the notice to quit or filed the complaint to retaliate against defendant.
   f. ☐ By serving defendant with the notice to quit or filing the complaint, plaintiff is arbitrarily discriminating against the defendant in violation of the Constitution or laws of the United States or California.
   g. ☐ Plaintiff's demand for possession violates the local rent control or eviction control ordinance of *(city or county, title of ordinance, and date of passage)*:

      (Also, briefly state the facts showing violation of the ordinance in item 3j.)
   h. ☐ Plaintiff accepted rent from defendant to cover a period of time after the date the notice to quit expired.
   i. ☐ Other affirmative defenses are stated in item 3j.

(Continued on reverse)

Form Approved by the
Judicial Council of California
982.1(95) [Rev. January 1, 1997]

ANSWER—Unlawful Detainer

Civil Code, § 1940 et seq.;
Code of Civil Procedure, § 425.12

PLAINTIFF (Name):	CASE NUMBER:
DEFENDANT (Name):	

3. AFFIRMATIVE DEFENSES (cont'd)

j. Facts supporting affirmative defenses checked above (identify each item separately by its letter from page one):

4. OTHER STATEMENTS

- a. ☐ Defendant vacated the premises on (date):
- b. ☐ The fair rental value of the premises alleged in the complaint is excessive (explain):
- c. ☐ Other (specify):

5. DEFENDANT REQUESTS

- a. that plaintiff take nothing requested in the complaint.
- b. costs incurred in this proceeding.
- c. ☐ reasonable attorney fees.
- d. ☐ that plaintiff be ordered to (1) make repairs and correct the conditions that constitute a breach of the warranty to provide habitable premises and (2) reduce the monthly rent to a reasonable rental value until the conditions are corrected.
- e. ☐ other (specify):

6. ☐ Number of pages attached (specify):

UNLAWFUL DETAINER ASSISTANT (Business and Professions Code sections 6400–6415)

7. (Must be completed in all cases) An unlawful detainer assistant ☐ did not ☐ did for compensation give advice or assistance with this form. (If defendant has received any help or advice for pay from an unlawful detainer assistant, state:)

- a. Assistant's name:
- b. Telephone No.:
- c. Street address, city, and ZIP:
- d. County of registration:
- e. Registration No.:
- f. Expires on (date):

▶ ....
(TYPE OR PRINT NAME)   (SIGNATURE OF DEFENDANT OR ATTORNEY)

▶ ....
(TYPE OR PRINT NAME)   (SIGNATURE OF DEFENDANT OR ATTORNEY)

(Each defendant for whom this answer is filed must be named in item 1 and must sign this answer unless his or her attorney signs.)

VERIFICATION

(Use a different verification form if the verification is by an attorney or for a corporation or partnership.)

I am the defendant in this proceeding and have read this answer. I declare under penalty of perjury under the laws of the State of California that the foregoing is true and correct.

Date:

▶ ....
(TYPE OR PRINT NAME)   (SIGNATURE OF DEFENDANT)

| ATTORNEY OR PARTY WITHOUT ATTORNEY *(Name and Address):* | TEL. NO.: | UNLAWFUL DETAINER ASSISTANT *(Check one box):* An unlawful detainer assistant ☐ did ☐ did not for compensation give advice or assistance with this form. *(If one did, state the following):* |

ASSISTANT'S NAME:

ADDRESS:

ATTORNEY FOR *(Name):*

NAME OF COURT AND JUDICIAL DISTRICT AND BRANCH COURT, IF ANY:

TEL. NO.:

COUNTY OF REGISTRATION:

REGISTRATION NO.:

SHORT TITLE OF CASE:

EXPIRES *(DATE):*

FORM INTERROGATORIES — UNLAWFUL DETAINER

Asking Party:

Answering Party:

Set No.:

CASE NUMBER:

Sec. 1. Instructions to All Parties

(a) These are general instructions. *For time limitations, requirements for service on other parties, and other details, see Code of Civil Procedure section 2030 and the cases construing it.*

(b) These interrogatories do not change existing law relating to interrogatories nor do they affect an answering party's right to assert any privilege or objection.

Sec. 2. Instructions to the Asking Party

(a) These interrogatories are designed for optional use in unlawful detainer proceedings.

(b) There are restrictions that generally limit the number of interrogatories that may be asked and the form and use of the interrogatories. For details, read Code of Civil Procedure section 2030(c).

(c) In determining whether to use these or any interrogatories, you should be aware that abuse can be punished by sanctions, including fines and attorney fees. See Code of Civil Procedure sections 128.5 and 128.7.

(d) Check the box next to each interrogatory that you want the answering party to answer. Use care in choosing those interrogatories that are applicable to the case.

(e) Additional interrogatories may be attached.

Sec. 3. Instructions to the Answering Party

(a) An answer or other appropriate response must be given to each interrogatory checked by the asking party. Failure to respond to these interrogatories properly can be punished by sanctions, including contempt proceedings, fine, attorneys fees, and the loss of your case. See Code of Civil Procedure sections 128.5, 128.7, and 2030.

(b) As a general rule, within five days after you are served with these interrogatories, you must serve your responses on the asking party and serve copies of your responses on all other parties to the action who have appeared. See Code Of Civil Procedure section 2030 for details.

(c) Each answer must be as complete and straightforward as the information reasonably available to you permits. If an interrogatory cannot be answered completely, answer it to the extent possible.

(d) If you do not have enough personal knowledge to fully answer an interrogatory, say so, but make a reasonable and good faith effort to get the information by asking other persons or organizations, unless the information is equally available to the asking party.

(e) Whenever an interrogatory may be answered by referring to a document, the document may be attached as an exhibit to the response and referred to in the response. If the document has more than one page, refer to the page and section where the answer to the interrogatory can be found.

(f) Whenever an address and telephone number for the same person are requested in more than one interrogatory, you are required to furnish them in answering only the first interrogatory asking for that information.

(g) Your answers to these interrogatories must be verified, dated, and signed. You may wish to use the following form *at the end of your answers:*

"I declare under penalty of perjury under the laws of the State of California that the foregoing answers are true and correct.

_____   _____
(DATE)   (SIGNATURE)

Sec. 4. Definitions

Words in **BOLDFACE CAPITALS** in these interrogatories are defined as follows:

(a) **PERSON** includes a natural person, firm, association, organization, partnership, business, trust, corporation, or public entity.

(b) **PLAINTIFF** includes any **PERSON** who seeks recovery of the **RENTAL UNIT** whether acting as an individual or on someone's behalf and includes all such **PERSONS** if more than one.

(Continued)

Form Approved by the
Judicial Council of California
FI-128 [Rev. July 1, 1987]
[Page 1 revised July 1, 1996]

**FORM INTERROGATORIES
UNLAWFUL DETAINER**

CCP 2030, 2033.5

(c) **LANDLORD** includes any **PERSON** who offered the **RENTAL UNIT** for rent and any **PERSON** on whose behalf the **RENTAL UNIT** was offered for rent and their successors in interest. **LANDLORD** includes all **PERSONS** who managed the **PROPERTY** while defendant was in possession.

(d) **RENTAL UNIT** is the premises **PLAINTIFF** seeks to recover.

(e) **PROPERTY** is the building or parcel (including common areas) of which the **RENTAL UNIT** is a part. (For example, if **PLAINTIFF** is seeking to recover possession of apartment number 12 of a 20-unit building, the building is the **PROPERTY** and apartment 12 is the **RENTAL UNIT**. If **PLAINTIFF** seeks possession of cottage number 3 in a five-cottage court or complex, the court or complex is the **PROPERTY** and cottage 3 is the **RENTAL UNIT**.)

(f) **DOCUMENT** means a writing, as defined in Evidence Code section 250, and includes the original or a copy of handwriting, typewriting, printing, photostating, photographing, and every other means of recording upon any tangible thing and form of communicating or representation, including letters, words, pictures, sounds, or symbols, or combinations of them.

(g) **NOTICE TO QUIT** includes the original or copy of any notice mentioned in Code of Civil Procedure section 1161 or Civil Code section 1946, including a 3-day notice to pay rent and quit the **RENTAL UNIT**, a 3-day notice to perform conditions or covenants or quit, a 3-day notice to quit, and a 30-day notice of termination.

(h) **ADDRESS** means the street address, including the city, state, and zip code.

Sec. 5. Interrogatories

The following interrogatories have been approved by the Judicial Council under section 2033.5 of the Code of Civil Procedure for use in unlawful detainer proceedings:

CONTENTS

70.0 General
71.0 Notice
72.0 Service
73.0 Malicious Holding Over
74.0 Rent Control and Eviction Control
75.0 Breach of Warranty to Provide Habitable Premises
76.0 Waiver, Change, Withdrawal, or Cancellation of Notice to Quit
77.0 Retaliation and Arbitrary Discrimination
78.0 Nonperformance of the Rental Agreement by Landlord
79.0 Offer of Rent by Defendant
80.0 Deduction from Rent for Necessary Repairs
81.0 Fair Market Rental Value

70.0 General

[Either party may ask any applicable question in this section.]

[ ] 70.1 State the name, **ADDRESS**, telephone number, and relationship to you of each **PERSON** who prepared or assisted in the preparation of the responses to these interrogatories. (Do not identify anyone who simply typed or reproduced the responses.)

[ ] 70.2 Is **PLAINTIFF** an owner of the **RENTAL UNIT**? If so, state:
(a) the nature and percentage of ownership interest;
(b) the date **PLAINTIFF** first acquired this ownership interest.

[ ] 70.3 Does **PLAINTIFF** share ownership or lack ownership? If so, state the name, the **ADDRESS**, and the nature and percentage of ownership interest of each owner.

[ ] 70.4 Does **PLAINTIFF** claim the right to possession other than as an owner of the **RENTAL UNIT**? If so, state the basis of the claim.

[ ] 70.5 Has **PLAINTIFF'S** interest in the **RENTAL UNIT** changed since acquisition? If so, state the nature and dates of each change.

[ ] 70.6 Are there other rental units on the **PROPERTY**? If so, state how many.

[ ] 70.7 During the 12 months before this proceeding was filed, did **PLAINTIFF** possess a permit or certificate of occupancy for the **RENTAL UNIT**? If so, for each state:
(a) the name and **ADDRESS** of each **PERSON** named on the permit or certificate;
(b) the dates of issuance and expiration;
(c) the permit or certificate number.

[ ] 70.8 Has a last month's rent, security deposit, cleaning fee, rental agency fee, credit check fee, key deposit, or any other deposit been paid on the **RENTAL UNIT**? If so, for each item state:
(a) the purpose of the payment;
(b) the date paid;
(c) the amount;
(d) the form of payment;
(e) the name of the **PERSON** paying;
(f) the name of the **PERSON** to whom it was paid;
(g) (any) **DOCUMENT** which evidences payment and the name, **ADDRESS**, and telephone number of each **PERSON** who has the **DOCUMENT**;
(h) any adjustments or deductions including facts.

[ ] (g) 70.9 State the date defendant first took possession of the **RENTAL UNIT**.

[ ] 70.10 State the date and all the terms of any rental agreement between defendant and the **PERSON** who rented to defendant.

[ ] 70.11 For each agreement alleged in the pleadings:
(a) identify all **DOCUMENTS** that are part of the agreement and for each state the name, the **ADDRESS**, and telephone number of each **PERSON** who has the **DOCUMENT**;
(b) state each part of the agreement not in writing, the name, **ADDRESS**, and telephone number of each **PERSON** agreeing to that provision, and the date that part of the agreement was made;
(c) identify all **DOCUMENTS** that evidence each part of the agreement not in writing and for each state the name, **ADDRESS**, and telephone number of each **PERSON** who has the **DOCUMENT**;
(d) identify all **DOCUMENTS** that are part of each modification to the agreement, and for each state

the name, **ADDRESS**, and telephone number of each **PERSON** who has the **DOCUMENT** (see also § 71.5);

(e) state each modification not in writing, the date, and the name, **ADDRESS**, and telephone number of the **PERSON** agreeing to the modification, and the date the modification was made (see also § 71.5);

(f) identify all **DOCUMENTS** that evidence each modification of the agreement not in writing and for each state the name, **ADDRESS**, and telephone number of each **PERSON** who has the **DOCUMENT** (see also § 71.5).

☐ 70.12 Has any **PERSON** acting on the **PLAINTIFF'S** behalf been responsible for any aspect of managing or maintaining the **RENTAL UNIT** or **PROPERTY**? If so, for each **PERSON** state:
(a) the name, **ADDRESS**, and telephone number;
(b) the dates the **PERSON** managed or maintained the **RENTAL UNIT** or P**ROPERTY**;
(c) the PERSON'S responsibilities.

☐ 70.13 For each **PERSON** who occupies any part of the **RENTAL UNIT** (except occupants named in the complaint and occupants' children under 17) state:

(a) the name, **ADDRESS**, telephone number, and birthdate;

(b) the inclusive dates of occupancy;

(c) a description of the portion of the **RENTAL UNIT** occupied;

(d) the amount paid, the term for which it was paid, and the person to whom it was paid;

(e) the nature of the use of the **RENTAL UNIT**;

(f) the name, **ADDRESS**, and telephone number of the person who authorized occupancy;

(g) how occupancy was authorized, including failure of the **LANDLORD** or **PLAINTIFF** to protest after discovering the occupancy.

☐ 70.14 Have you or anyone acting on your behalf obtained any **DOCUMENT** concerning the tenancy between any occupant of the **RENTAL UNIT** and any **PERSON** with an ownership interest or managerial responsibility for the **RENTAL UNIT**? If so, for each **DOCUMENT** state:

(a) the name, **ADDRESS**, and telephone number of each individual from whom the **DOCUMENT** was obtained;

(b) the name, **ADDRESS**, and telephone number of each individual who obtained the **DOCUMENT**;

(c) the date the **DOCUMENT** was obtained;

(d) the name, **ADDRESS**, and telephone number of each **PERSON** who has the **DOCUMENT** (original or copy).

71.0 Notice

[If a defense is based on allegations that the 3-day notice or 30-day NOTICE TO QUIT is defective in form or content, then either party may ask any applicable question in this section.]

☐ 71.1 Was the **NOTICE TO QUIT** on which **PLAINTIFF** bases this proceeding attached to the complaint? If not, state the contents of this notice.

☐ 71.2 State all reasons that the **NOTICE TO QUIT** was served and for each reason:

(a) state all facts supporting **PLAINTIFF'S** decision to terminate defendant's tenancy;

(b) state the names, **ADDRESSES**, and telephone numbers of all **PERSONS** who have knowledge of the facts;

(c) identify all **DOCUMENTS** that support the facts and state the name, **ADDRESS**, and telephone number of each **PERSON** who has each **DOCUMENT**.

☐ 71.3 List all rent payments and rent credits made or claimed by or on behalf of defendant beginning 12 months before the **NOTICE TO QUIT** was served. For each payment or credit state:
(a) the amount;
(b) the date received;
(c) the form in which any payment was made;
(d) the services performed or other basis for which a credit is claimed;
(e) the period covered;
(f) the name of each **PERSON** making the payment or earning the credit;
(g) the identity of all **DOCUMENTS** evidencing the payment or credit and for each state the name, **ADDRESS**, and telephone number of each **PERSON** who has the **DOCUMENT**.

☐ 71.4 Did defendant ever fail to pay the rent on time? If so, for each late payment state:
(a) the date;
(b) the amount of any late charge;
(c) the identity of all **DOCUMENTS** recording the payment and for each state the name, **ADDRESS**, and telephone number of each **PERSON** who has the **DOCUMENT**.

☐ 71.5 Since the beginning of defendant's tenancy, has **PLAINTIFF** ever raised the rent? If so, for each rent increase state:
(a) the date the increase became effective;
(b) the amount;
(c) the reasons for the rent increase;
(d) how and when defendant was notified of the increase;
(e) the identity of all **DOCUMENTS** evidencing the increase and for each state the name, **ADDRESS**, and telephone number of each **PERSON** who has the **DOCUMENT**.

[See also section 70.11(d)–(f).]

☐ 71.6 During the 12 months before the **NOTICE TO QUIT** was served was there a period during which there was no permit or certificate of occupancy for the **RENTAL UNIT**? If so, for each period state:
(a) the inclusive dates;
(b) the reasons.

☐ 71.7 Has any **PERSON** ever reported any nuisance or disturbance at or destruction of the **RENTAL UNIT** or **PROPERTY** caused by defendant or other occupant of the **RENTAL UNIT** or their guests? If so, for each report state;
(a) a description of the disturbance or destruction;
(b) the date of the report;
(c) the name of the **PERSON** who reported;
(d) the name of the **PERSON** to whom the report was made;
(e) what action was taken as a result of the report;
(f) the identity of all **DOCUMENTS** evidencing the report and for each state the name, **ADDRESS**, and telephone number of each **PERSON** who has each **DOCUMENT**.

☐ 71.8 Does the complaint allege violation of a term of a rental agreement or lease (other than nonpayment of rent)? If so, for each covenant:
(a) identify the covenant breached;
(b) state the facts supporting the allegation of a breach;
(c) state the names, ADDRESSES, and telephone numbers of all PERSONS who have knowledge of the facts;
(d) identify all DOCUMENTS that support the facts and state the name, ADDRESS, and telephone number of each PERSON who has each DOCUMENT.

☐ 71.9 Does the complaint allege that the defendant has been using the RENTAL UNIT for an illegal purpose? If so, for each illegal purpose:
(a) identify the illegal purpose;
(b) state the facts supporting the allegations of illegal use;
(c) state the names, ADDRESSES, and telephone numbers of all PERSONS who have knowledge of the facts;
(d) identify all DOCUMENTS that support the facts and state the name, ADDRESS, and telephone number of each PERSON who has each DOCUMENT.

[Additional interrogatories on this subject may be found in sections 75.0, 78.0, 79.0, and 80.0.]

72.0 Service

[If a defense is based on allegations that the NOTICE TO QUIT was defectively served, then either party may ask any applicable question in this section.]

☐ 72.1 Does defendant contend (or base a defense or make any allegations) that the NOTICE TO QUIT was defectively served? If the answer is "no," do not answer interrogatories 72.2 through 72.3.

☐ 72.2 Does PLAINTIFF contend that the NOTICE TO QUIT referred to in the complaint was served? If so, state:
(a) the kind of notice;
(b) the date and time of service;
(c) the manner of service;
(d) the name and ADDRESS of the person who served it;
(e) a description of any DOCUMENT or conversation between defendant and the person who served the notice.

☐ 72.3 Did any person receive the NOTICE TO QUIT referred to in the complaint? If so, for each copy of notice state:
(a) the name of the person who received it;
(b) the kind of notice;
(c) how it was delivered;
(d) the date received;
(e) where it was delivered;
(f) the identity of all DOCUMENTS evidencing the notice and for each state the name, ADDRESS, and telephone number of each PERSON who has the DOCUMENT.

73.0 Malicious Holding Over

[If a defendant denies that defendant's continued possession is malicious, then either party may ask any applicable question in this section. Additional questions in section 75.0 may also be applicable.]

☐ 73.1 If any rent called for by the rental agreement is unpaid, state the reasons and the facts upon which the reasons are based.

☐ 73.2 Has defendant made any attempts to secure other premises since the service of the NOTICE TO QUIT or premises since the service of the summons and complaint? If so, for each attempt:
(a) state all facts indicating the attempt to secure other premises;
(b) state the names, ADDRESSES, and telephone numbers of all PERSONS who have knowledge of the facts;
(c) identify all DOCUMENTS that support the facts and state the name, ADDRESS, and telephone number of each PERSON who has each DOCUMENT.

☐ 73.3 State the facts upon which PLAINTIFF bases the allegation of malice.

74.0 Rent Control and Eviction Control

☐ 74.1 Is there an ordinance or other local law in this jurisdiction which limits the right to evict tenants? If your answer is no, you need not answer sections 74.2 through 74.6.

☐ 74.2 For the ordinance or other local law limiting the right to evict tenants, state:
(a) the title or number of the law;
(b) the locality.

☐ 74.3 Do you contend that the RENTAL UNIT is exempt from the eviction provisions of the ordinance or other local law identified in section 74.2? If so, state the facts upon which you base your contention.

☐ 74.4 Is this proceeding based on allegations of a need to recover the RENTAL UNIT for use of the LANDLORD or the landlord's relative? If so, for each intended occupant state:
(a) the name;
(b) the residence ADDRESSES from three years ago to the present;
(c) the relationship to the LANDLORD;
(d) all the intended occupant's reasons for occupancy;
(e) all rental units on the PROPERTY that were vacated within 60 days before and after the date the NOTICE TO QUIT was served.

☐ 74.5 Is the proceeding based on an allegation that the LANDLORD wishes to remove the RENTAL UNIT from residential use temporarily or permanently (for example, to rehabilitate, demolish, renovate, or convert)? If so, state:
(a) each reason for removing the RENTAL UNIT from residential use;
(b) what physical changes and renovation will be made to the RENTAL UNIT;
(c) the date the work is to begin and end;
(d) the number, date, and type of each permit for the change of work;

(e) the identity of each **DOCUMENT** evidencing the intended activity (for example, blueprints, plans, applications for financing, construction contracts) and the name, **ADDRESS**, and telephone number of each **PERSON** who has each **DOCUMENT**.

☐ 74.6 Is the proceeding based on any ground other than those stated in sections 74.4 and 74.5? If so, for each:

(a) state each fact supporting or opposing the ground;

(b) state the names, **ADDRESSES**, and telephone numbers of all **PERSONS** who have knowledge of the facts;

(c) identify all **DOCUMENTS** evidencing the facts and state the name, **ADDRESS**, and telephone number of each **PERSON** who has each **DOCUMENT**.

75.0 Breach of Warranty to Provide Habitable Premises

[If plaintiff alleges nonpayment of rent and defendant bases his defense on allegations of implied or express breach of warranty to provide habitable residential premises, then either party may ask any applicable question in this section.]

☐ 75.1 Do you know of any conditions in violation of state or local building codes, housing codes, or health codes, conditions of dilapidation, or other conditions in need of repair in the **RENTAL UNIT** or on the **PROPERTY** that affected the **RENTAL UNIT** at any time defendant has been in possession? If so, state:

(a) the type of condition;

(b) the kind if corrections or repairs needed;

(c) how and when you learned of these conditions;

(d) how these conditions were caused;

(e) the name, **ADDRESS**, and telephone number of each **PERSON** who has caused these conditions.

☐ 75.2 Have any corrections, repairs, or improvements been made to the **RENTAL UNIT** since the **RENTAL UNIT** was rented to defendant? If so, for each correction, repair, or improvement state:

(a) a description giving the nature and location;

(b) the date;

(c) the name, **ADDRESS**, and telephone number of each **PERSON** who made the repairs or improvements;

(d) the cost;

(e) the identity of any **DOCUMENT** evidencing the repairs or improvements;

(f) if a building permit was issued, state the issuing agencies and the permit number of your copy.

☐ 75.3 Did defendant or any other **PERSON** during 36 months before the **NOTICE TO QUIT** was served or during defendant's possession of the **RENTAL UNIT** notify the **LANDLORD** or his agent or employee about the condition of the **RENTAL UNIT** or **PROPERTY**? If so, for each written or oral notice state:

(a) the substance;

(b) who made it;

(c) when and how it was made;

(d) the name and **ADDRESS** of each **PERSON** to whom it was made;

(e) the name and **ADDRESS** of each person who knows about it;

(f) the identity of each **DOCUMENT** evidencing the and the name, **ADDRESS**, and telephone number of each **PERSON** who has it;

(g) the response made to the notice;

(h) the efforts made to correct the conditions;

(i) whether the **PERSON** who gave notice was an occupant of the **PROPERTY** at the time of the complaint.

☐ 75.4 During the period beginning 36 months before the **NOTICE TO QUIT** was served to the present, was the **RENTAL UNIT** or **PROPERTY** (including other rental units) inspected for dilapidations or defective conditions by a representative of any governmental agency? If so, for each inspection state:

(a) the date;

(b) the reason;

(c) the name of the governmental agency;

(d) the name, **ADDRESS**, and telephone number of each inspector;

(e) the identity of each **DOCUMENT** evidencing each inspection and the name, **ADDRESS**, and telephone number of each **PERSON** who has it.

☐ 75.5 During the period beginning 36 months before the **NOTICE TO QUIT** was served to the present, did **PLAINTIFF** or **LANDLORD** receive a notice or other communication regarding the condition of the **RENTAL UNIT** or **PROPERTY** (including other rental units) from a governmental agency? If so, for each notice or communication state:

(a) the date received;

(b) the identity of all parties;

(c) the substance of the notice or communication;

(d) the identity of each **DOCUMENT** evidencing the notice or communication and the name, **ADDRESS**, and telephone number of each **PERSON** who has it.

☐ 75.6 Was there any corrective action taken in response to the inspection or notice or communication identified in sections 75.4 and 75.5? If so, for each:

(a) identify the notice or communication;

(b) identify the condition;

(c) describe the corrective action;

(d) identify of each **DOCUMENT** evidencing the corrective action and the name, **ADDRESS**, and telephone number of each **PERSON** who has it.

☐ 75.7 Has the **PROPERTY** been appraised for sale or loan during the period beginning 36 months before the **NOTICE TO QUIT** was served to the present? If so, for each appraisal state:

(a) the date;

(b) the name, **ADDRESS**, and telephone number of the appraisal

(c) the purpose of the appraisal;

(d) the identity of each **DOCUMENT** evidencing the appraisal and the name, **ADDRESS**, and telephone number of each **PERSON** who has it.

☐ 75.8 Was any condition requiring repair or correction at the **PROPERTY** or **RENTAL UNIT** caused by defendant or other occupant of the **RENTAL UNIT** or their guests? If so, state:

(a) the type and location of condition;

(b) the kind of corrections or repairs needed;

(c) how and when you learned of these conditions;

(d) how and when these conditions were caused;

(e) the name, **ADDRESS**, and telephone number of each **PERSON** who caused these conditions;

(f) the identity of each **DOCUMENT** evidencing the repair (or correction) and the name, **ADDRESS**, and telephone number of each **PERSON** who has it.

[See also section 71.0 for additional questions.]

76.0 Waiver, Change, Withdrawal, or Cancellation of Notice to Quit

[If a defense is based on waiver, change, withdrawal, or cancellation of the NOTICE TO QUIT, then either party may ask any applicable question in this section.]

☐ 76.1 Did the **PLAINTIFF** or **LANDLORD** or anyone acting on his or her behalf do anything which is alleged to have been a waiver, change, withdrawal, or cancellation of the **NOTICE TO QUIT**? If so:
(a) state the facts supporting this allegation;
(b) state the names, **ADDRESSES**, and telephone numbers of all **PERSONS** who have knowledge of these facts;
(c) identify each **DOCUMENT** that supports the fact sand state the name, **ADDRESS**, and telephone number of each **PERSON** who has it.

☐ 76.2 Did the **PLAINTIFF** or **LANDLORD** accept rent which covered a period after the date for vacating the **RENTAL UNIT** as specified in the **NOTICE TO QUIT**? If so:
(a) state the facts;
(b) state the names, **ADDRESSES**, and telephone numbers of all **PERSONS** who have knowledge of the facts;
(c) identify each **DOCUMENT** that supports the facts and state the name, **ADDRESS**, and telephone number of each **PERSON** who has it.

77.0 Retaliation and Arbitrary Discrimination

[If a defense is based on retaliation or arbitrary discrimination, then either party may ask any applicable question in this section.]

☐ 77.1 State all reasons that the **NOTICE TO QUIT** was served or that defendant's tenancy was not renewed and for each reason:
(a) state all facts supporting **PLAINTIFF'S** decision to terminate or not renew defendant's tenancy;
(b) state the names, **ADDRESSES**, and telephone numbers of all **PERSONS** who have knowledge of the facts;
(c) identify all **DOCUMENTS** that support the facts and state the name, **ADDRESS**, and telephone number of each **PERSON** who has it.

78.0 Nonperformance of the Rental Agreement by Landlord

[If a defense is based on nonperformance of the rental agreement by the LANDLORD or someone acting on the LANDLORD'S behalf, then either party may ask any applicable question in this section.]

☐ 78.1 Did the **LANDLORD** or anyone acting on the **LANDLORD'S** behalf agree to make repairs, alterations, or improvements at any time or provide services to the **PROPERTY** or **RENTAL UNIT**? If so, for each agreement state:
(a) the substance of the agreement;

(b) when it was made;
(c) whether it was written or oral;
(d) by whom and to whom;
(e) the name and ADDRESS of each person who knows about it;
(f) whether all promised repairs, alterations, or improvements were completed or services provided;
(g) the reasons for any failure to perform;
(h) the identity of each **DOCUMENT** evidencing the agreement or promise and the name, **ADDRESS**, and telephone number of each **PERSON** who has it.

☐ 78.2 Has **PLAINTIFF** or **LANDLORD** or any resident of the **PROPERTY** ever committed disturbances or interfered with the quiet enjoyment of the **RENTAL UNIT** (including, for example, noise, acts which threaten the loss of title to the property or loss of financing, etc.)? If so, for each disturbance or interference, state:
(a) a description of each act;
(b) the date of each act;
(c) the name, **ADDRESS**, and telephone number of each **PERSON** who acted;
(d) the name, **ADDRESS**, and telephone number of each **PERSON** who witnessed each act and any **DOCUMENTS** evidencing the person's knowledge;
(e) what action was taken by the **PLAINTIFF** or **LANDLORD** to end or lessen the disturbance or interference.

79.0 Offer of Rent by Defendant

[If a defense is based on an offer of rent by a defendant which was refused, then either party may ask any applicable question in this section.]

☐ 79.1 Has defendant or anyone acting on the defendant's behalf offered any payments to **PLAINTIFF** which **PLAINTIFF** refused to accept? If so, for each offer state:
(a) the amount;
(b) the date;
(c) purpose of offer;
(d) the manner of the offer;
(e) the identity of the person making the offer;
(f) the identity of the person refusing the offer;
(g) the date of the refusal;
(h) the reasons for the refusal.

80.0 Deduction from Rent for Necessary Repairs

[If a defense to payment of rent or damages is based on claim of retaliatory eviction, then either party may ask any applicable question in this section. Additional questions in section 75.0 may also be applicable.]

☐ 80.1 Does defendant claim to have deducted from rent any amount which was withheld to make repairs after communication to the **LANDLORD** of the need for the repairs? If the answer is "no," do not answer interrogatories 80.2 through 80.6.

☐ 80.2 For each condition in need of repair for which a deduction was made, state:
(a) the nature of the condition;
(b) the location;
(c) the date the condition was discovered by defendant;
(d) the date the condition was first known by **LANDLORD** or **PLAINTIFF**;

(e) the dates and methods of each notice to the **LANDLORD** or **PLAINTIFF** of the condition;

(f) the response or action taken by the **LANDLORD** or **PLAINTIFF** to each notification;

(g) the cost to remedy the condition and how the cost was determined;

(h) the identity of any bids obtained for the repairs and any **DOCUMENTS** evidencing the bids.

☐ 80.3 Did **LANDLORD** or **PLAINTIFF** fail to respond within a reasonable time after receiving a communication of a need for repair? If so, for each communication state:
(a) the date it was made;
(b) how it was made;
(c) the response and date;
(d) why the delay was unreasonable.

☐ 80.4 Was there an insufficient period specified or actually allowed between the time of notification and the time repairs were begun by defendant to allow **LANDLORD** or **PLAINTIFF** to make the repairs? If so, state all facts on which the claim of insufficiency is based.

☐ 80.5 Does **PLAINTIFF** contend that any of the items for which rent deductions were taken were not allowable under law? If so, for each item state all reasons and facts on which you base your contention.

☐ 80.6 Has defendant vacated or does defendant anticipate vacating the **RENTAL UNIT** because repairs were requested and not made within a reasonable time? If so, state all facts on which defendant justifies having vacated the **RENTAL UNIT** or anticipates vacating the rental unit.

81.0 Fair Market Rental Value

*[If defendant denies PLAINTIFF allegation on the fair market rental value of the **RENTAL UNIT**, then either party may ask any applicable question in this section. If defendant claims that the fair market rental value is less because of a breach of warranty to provide habitable premises, then either party may also ask any applicable question in section 75.0]*

☐ 81.1 Do you have an opinion on the fair market rental value of the **RENTAL UNIT**? If so, state:
(a) the substance of your opinion;
(b) the factors upon which the fair market rental value is based;
(c) the method used to calculate the fair market rental value.

☐ 81.2 Has any other **PERSON** ever expressed to you an opinion on the fair market rental value of the **RENTAL UNIT**? If so, for each **PERSON**:

(a) state the name, **ADDRESS**, and telephone number;
(b) state the substance of the **PERSON**'s opinion;
(c) describe the conversation or identify all **DOCUMENTS** in which the **PERSON** expressed an opinion and state the name, **ADDRESS**, and telephone number of each **PERSON** who has each **DOCUMENT**.

☐ 81.3 Do you know of any current violations of state or local building codes, housing codes, or health codes, conditions of dilapidation or other conditions in need of repair in the **RENTAL UNIT** or common areas that have affected the **RENTAL UNIT** at any time defendant has been in possession? If so, state:
(a) the conditions in need of repair;
(b) the kind of repairs needed;
(c) the name, **ADDRESS**, and telephone number of each **PERSON** who caused these conditions.

This page intentionally left blank.

ATTORNEY OR PARTY WITHOUT ATTORNEY *(Name, state bar number, and address):*	*FOR COURT USE ONLY*

TELEPHONE NO.:   FAX NO. *(Optional):*

E-MAIL ADDRESS *(Optional):*

ATTORNEY FOR *(Name):*

SUPERIOR COURT OF CALIFORNIA, COUNTY OF

STREET ADDRESS:

MAILING ADDRESS:

CITY AND ZIP CODE:

BRANCH NAME:

PLAINTIFF:

DEFENDANT:

JUDGMENT

☐ **By Clerk** ☐ **By Default** ☐ **After Court Trial**
☐ **By Court** ☐ **On Stipulation** ☐ **Defendant Did Not Appear at Trial**

CASE NUMBER:

JUDGMENT

1. ☐ **BY DEFAULT**
   a. Defendant was properly served with a copy of the summons and complaint.
   b. Defendant failed to answer the complaint or appear and defend the action within the time allowed by law.
   c. Defendant's default was entered by the clerk upon plaintiff's application.
   d. ☐ **Clerk's Judgment** (Code Civ. Proc., § 585(a)). Defendant was sued only on a contract or judgment of a court of this state for the recovery of money.
   e. ☐ **Court Judgment** (Code Civ. Proc., § 585(b)). The court considered
      (1) ☐ plaintiff's testimony and other evidence.
      (2) ☐ plaintiff's written declaration (Code Civ. Proc., § 585(d)).

2. ☐ **ON STIPULATION**
   a. Plaintiff and defendant agreed (stipulated) that a judgment be entered in this case. The court approved the stipulated judgment and
   b. ☐ the signed written stipulation was filed in the case.
   c. ☐ the stipulation was stated in open court ☐ the stipulation was stated on the record.

3. ☐ **AFTER COURT TRIAL.** The jury was waived. The court considered the evidence.
   a. The case was tried on *(date and time):*
      before *(name of judicial officer):*
   b. Appearances by:
      ☐ Plaintiff *(name each):*   ☐ Plaintiff's attorney *(name each):*
        (1)   (1)
        (2)   (2)
      ☐ Continued on Attachment 3b.

      ☐ Defendant *(name each):*   ☐ Defendant 's attorney *(name each):*
        (1)   (1)
        (2)   (2)
      ☐ Continued on Attachment 3b.

   c. ☐ Defendant did not appear at trial. Defendant was properly served with notice of trial.

   d. ☐ A statement of decision (Code Civ. Proc., § 632) ☐ was not ☐ was requested.

Page 1 of 2

JUDGMENT IS ENTERED AS FOLLOWS BY: ☐ **THE COURT** ☐ **THE CLERK**

4. ☐ **Stipulated Judgment.** Judgment is entered according to the stipulation of the parties.

5. **Parties.** Judgment is

    a. ☐ for plaintiff *(name each):*

        and against defendant *(names):*

        ☐ Continued on Attachment 5a.

    b. ☐ for defendant *(name each):*

    c. ☐ for cross-complainant *(name each):*

        and against cross-defendant *(name each):*

        ☐ Continued on Attachment 5c.

    d. ☐ for cross-defendant *(name each):*

6. **Amount.**

    a. ☐ Defendant named in item 5a above must pay plaintiff on the complaint:

(1) ☐ Damages	$
(2) ☐ Prejudgment interest at the annual rate of %	$
(3) ☐ Attorney fees	$
(4) ☐ Costs	$
(5) ☐ Other *(specify):*	$
(6) **TOTAL**	$

    c. ☐ Cross-defendant named in item 5c above must pay cross-complainant on the cross-complaint:

(1) ☐ Damages	$
(2) ☐ Prejudgment interest at the annual rate of %	$
(3) ☐ Attorney fees	$
(4) ☐ Costs	$
(5) ☐ Other *(specify):*	$
(6) **TOTAL**	$

    b. ☐ Plaintiff to receive nothing from defendant named in item 5b.
        ☐ Defendant named in item 5b to recover costs $
            ☐ and attorney fees $

    d. ☐ Cross-complainant to receive nothing from cross-defendant named in item 5d.
        ☐ Cross-defendant named in item 5d to recover costs $
            ☐ and attorney fees $

7. ☐ Other *(specify):*

Date: _____

☐ _____
JUDICIAL OFFICER

Date: _____

☐ Clerk, by _____ , Deputy

(SEAL)

CLERK'S CERTIFICATE *(Optional)*

I certify that this is a true copy of the original judgment on file in the court.

Date:

Clerk, by _____ , Deputy

Page 2 of 2

JUDGMENT

Preliminary Lien Notice

TO   _____
                        (occupant)

           _____
                        (address)

           _____
                        (state)

You owe and have not paid rent and/or other charges for the use of storage _____ (space number) at _____ (name and address of storage facility). These charges total $ _____ (amount) and have been due for more than 14 days. They are itemized as follows:

Due Date	Description	Amount

                                                 TOTAL: $ _____

If this sum is not paid in full before _____ (date at least 14 days from mailing) your right to use the storage space will terminate, you will be denied access, and an owner's lien on any stored property will be imposed.

You may pay this sum and may contact the owner at:

_____
                (name)

_____
              (address)

_____
                (state)

_____
            (telephone)

_____
                (date)

                                         _____
                                              (owner's signature)

This page intentionally left blank.

THREE DAY/SIXTY DAY NOTICE

THREE DAY NOTICE TO PAY RENT OR QUIT

TO _____

And all other tenants, subtenants, and others in possession of the property located at:

Address _____ Space number _____

City of _____ County of _____

State of California

Rent on the above described property is due and owing from _____ *(date)* in the amount of $ _____.

You are required to pay the amount owing in full within three (3) days after the service of this notice to _____ *(Owner/Agent/Park Manager)* or quit and deliver possession of the premises to the above party.

Failure to deliver up the premises will result in legal action against you to recover all monies owed as well as the premises and all other damages allowed by law. Failure to pay the money owed will also result in the termination of your lease/rental agreement.

You are also notified that negative information may be submitted to a credit reporting agency which may result in a negative credit report if you fail to meet your financial obligations.

_____   _____
             Owner/Agent   Date

NOTICE OF TERMINATION OF TENANCY

TO _____

And all other tenants, subtenants, and others in possession of the property located at:

Address _____ _____ Space number _____

City of _____ County of _____

State of California

This notice to you that your tenancy of space number _____ at _____

_____ *(address)*, in the City of _____,

County of _____, California is terminated and that your mobile home must be removed from the above address not later than _____ *(Date more than 60 days after receipt of notice)*.

Reason(s) for termination *(Detail all reasons for termination)*: _____

_____

_____

Signature _____   Date _____
                Owner/Agent

PROOF OF SERVICE

I, the undersigned, being at least 18 years of age, served this notice, of which this is a true copy, on _____, the person(s) named above. The notice was served by:

- ❏ Personal delivery of a copy to the above named person(s).
- ❏ Delivery of a copy for each of the above named to a person of suitable age and discretion at the above named person(s) residence/business after attempting to personally serve the above named person(s) at his/her/their residence and place of business (if known) and mailing by first class mail a second copy to his/her/their residence.
- ❏ Posting a copy for each of the above named person(s) in a conspicuous place on the above identified property, being unable to personally serve a person of suitable age or discretion at the residence or known place(s) of business of the above named person(s) and mailing on the same date by first class mail a second copy to each above named person(s) to the address of the above identified property.

I declare under penalty of perjury that the above proof of service is true and correct.

Name _____   Date _____

Index

SPHINX® PUBLISHING ORDER FORM

Qty	ISBN	Title	Retail	Ext.
		SPHINX PUBLISHING NATIONAL TITLES		
	1-57248-148-X	Cómo Hacer su Propio Testamento	$16.95	
	1-57248-226-5	Cómo Restablecer su propio Crédito y Renegociar sus Deudas	$21.95	
	1-57248-147-1	Cómo Solicitar su Propio Divorcio	$24.95	
	1-57248-238-9	The 529 College Savings Plan	$16.95	
	1-57248-166-8	The Complete Book of Corporate Forms	$24.95	
	1-57248-229-X	The Complete Legal Guide to Senior Care	$21.95	
	1-57248-201-X	The Complete Patent Book	$26.95	
	1-57248-163-3	Crime Victim's Guide to Justice (2E)	$21.95	
	1-57248-251-6	The Entrepreneur's Internet Handbook	$21.95	
	1-57248-159-5	Essential Guide to Real Estate Contracts	$18.95	
	1-57248-160-9	Essential Guide to Real Estate Leases	$18.95	
	1-57248-254-0	Family Limited Partnership	$26.95	
	1-57248-139-0	Grandparents' Rights (3E)	$24.95	
	1-57248-188-9	Guía de Inmigración a Estados Unidos (3E)	$24.95	
	1-57248-187-0	Guía de Justicia para Víctimas del Crimen	$21.95	
	1-57248-103-X	Help Your Lawyer Win Your Case (2E)	$14.95	
	1-57248-164-1	How to Buy a Condominium or Townhome (2E)	$19.95	
	1-57248-191-9	How to File Your Own Bankruptcy (5E)	$21.95	
	1-57248-132-3	How to File Your Own Divorce (4E)	$24.95	
	1-57248-083-1	How to Form a Limited Liability Company	$22.95	
	1-57248-231-1	How to Form a Nonprofit Corporation (2E)	$24.95	
	1-57248-133-1	How to Form Your Own Corporation (3E)	$24.95	
	1-57248-224-9	How to Form Your Own Partnership (2E)	$24.95	
	1-57248-232-X	How to Make Your Own Simple Will (3E)	$18.95	
	1-57248-200-1	How to Register Your Own Copyright (4E)	$24.95	
	1-57248-104-8	How to Register Your Own Trademark (3E)	$21.95	
	1-57248-233-8	How to Write Your Own Living Will (3E)	$18.95	
	1-57248-156-0	How to Write Your Own Premarital Agreement (3E)	$24.95	
	1-57248-230-3	Incorporate in Delaware from Any State	$24.95	
	1-57248-158-7	Incorporate in Nevada from Any State	$24.95	
	1-57248-250-8	Inmigración a los EE.UU. Paso a Paso	$22.95	
	1-57071-333-2	Jurors' Rights (2E)	$12.95	
	1-57248-223-0	Legal Research Made Easy (3E)	$21.95	
	1-57248-165-X	Living Trusts and Other Ways to Avoid Probate (3E)	$24.95	

Qty	ISBN	Title	Retail	Ext.
	1-57248-186-2	Manual de Beneficios para el Seguro Social	$18.95	
	1-57248-220-6	Mastering the MBE	$16.95	
	1-57248-167-6	Most Valuable Bus. Legal Forms You'll Ever Need (3E)	$21.95	
	1-57248-130-7	Most Valuable Personal Legal Forms You'll Ever Need	$24.95	
	1-57248-098-X	The Nanny and Domestic Help Legal Kit	$22.95	
	1-57248-089-0	Neighbor v. Neighbor (2E)	$16.95	
	1-57248-169-2	The Power of Attorney Handbook (4E)	$19.95	
	1-57248-149-8	Repair Your Own Credit and Deal with Debt	$18.95	
	1-57248-217-6	Sexual Harassment: Your Guide to Legal Action	$18.95	
	1-57248-219-2	The Small Business Owner's Guide to Bankruptcy	$21.95	
	1-57248-168-4	The Social Security Benefits Handbook (3E)	$18.95	
	1-57248-216-8	Social Security Q&A	$12.95	
	1-57248-221-4	Teen Rights	$22.95	
	1-57248-236-2	Unmarried Parents' Rights (2E)	$19.95	
	1-57248-161-7	U.S.A. Immigration Guide (4E)	$24.95	
	1-57248-192-7	The Visitation Handbook	$18.95	
	1-57248-225-7	Win Your Unemployment Compensation Claim (2E)	$21.95	
	1-57248-138-2	Winning Your Personal Injury Claim (2E)	$24.95	
	1-57248-162-5	Your Right to Child Custody, Visitation and Support (2E)	$24.95	
	1-57248-157-9	Your Rights When You Owe Too Much	$16.95	
		CALIFORNIA TITLES		
	1-57248-150-1	CA Power of Attorney Handbook (2E)	$18.95	
	1-57248-151-X	How to File for Divorce in CA (3E)	$26.95	
	1-57071-356-1	How to Make a CA Will	$16.95	
	1-57248-145-5	How to Probate and Settle an Estate in California	$26.95	
	1-57248-146-3	How to Start a Business in CA	$18.95	
	1-57248-194-3	How to Win in Small Claims Court in CA (2E)	$18.95	
	1-57248-196-X	The Landlord's Legal Guide in CA	$24.95	
	1-57248-241-9	Tenants' Rights in CA	$21.95	
		FLORIDA TITLES		
	1-57071-363-4	Florida Power of Attorney Handbook (2E)	$16.95	
	1-57248-176-5	How to File for Divorce in FL (7E)	$26.95	
	1-57248-177-3	How to Form a Corporation in FL (5E)	$24.95	
	1-57248-203-6	How to Form a Limited Liability Co. in FL (2E)	$24.95	
	1-57071-401-0	How to Form a Partnership in FL	$22.95	

Form Continued on Following Page   **SUBTOTAL**

SPHINX® PUBLISHING ORDER FORM

Qty	ISBN	Title	Retail	Ext.
	1-57248-113-7	How to Make a FL Will (6E)	$16.95	
	1-57248-088-2	How to Modify Your FL Divorce Judgment (4E)	$24.95	
	1-57248-144-7	How to Probate and Settle an Estate in FL (4E)	$26.95	
	1-57248-081-5	How to Start a Business in FL (5E)	$16.95	
	1-57248-204-4	How to Win in Small Claims Court in FL (7E)	$18.95	
	1-57248-202-8	Land Trusts in Florida (6E)	$29.95	
	1-57248-123-4	Landlords' Rights and Duties in FL (8E)	$21.95	

GEORGIA TITLES

Qty	ISBN	Title	Retail	Ext.
	1-57248-137-4	How to File for Divorce in GA (4E)	$21.95	
	1-57248-180-3	How to Make a GA Will (4E)	$21.95	
	1-57248-140-4	How to Start a Business in Georgia (2E)	$16.95	

ILLINOIS TITLES

Qty	ISBN	Title	Retail	Ext.
	1-57248-244-3	Child Custody, Visitation, and Support in IL	$24.95	
	1-57248-206-0	How to File for Divorce in IL (3E)	$24.95	
	1-57248-170-6	How to Make an IL Will (3E)	$16.95	
	1-57248-247-8	How to Start a Business in IL (3E)	$21.95	
	1-57248-252-4	The Landlord's Legal Guide in IL	$24.95	

MASSACHUSETTS TITLES

Qty	ISBN	Title	Retail	Ext.
	1-57248-128-5	How to File for Divorce in MA (3E)	$24.95	
	1-57248-115-3	How to Form a Corporation in MA	$24.95	
	1-57248-108-0	How to Make a MA Will (2E)	$16.95	
	1-57248-248-6	How to Start a Business in MA (3E)	$21.95	
	1-57248-209-5	The Landlord's Legal Guide in MA	$24.95	

MICHIGAN TITLES

Qty	ISBN	Title	Retail	Ext.
	1-57248-215-X	How to File for Divorce in MI (3E)	$24.95	
	1-57248-182-X	How to Make a MI Will (3E)	$16.95	
	1-57248-183-8	How to Start a Business in MI (3E)	$18.95	

MINNESOTA TITLES

Qty	ISBN	Title	Retail	Ext.
	1-57248-142-0	How to File for Divorce in MN	$21.95	
	1-57248-179-X	How to Form a Corporation in MN	$24.95	
	1-57248-178-1	How to Make a MN Will (2E)	$16.95	

NEW YORK TITLES

Qty	ISBN	Title	Retail	Ext.
	1-57248-193-5	Child Custody, Visitation and Support in NY	$26.95	
	1-57248-141-2	How to File for Divorce in NY (2E)	$26.95	
	1-57248-249-4	How to Form a Corporation in NY (2E)	$24.95	
	1-57248-095-5	How to Make a NY Will (2E)	$16.95	
	1-57248-199-4	How to Start a Business in NY (2E)	$18.95	

Qty	ISBN	Title	Retail	Ext.
	1-57248-198-6	How to Win in Small Claims Court in NY (2E)	$18.95	
	1-57248-197-8	Landlords' Legal Guide in NY	$24.95	
	1-57071-188-7	New York Power of Attorney Handbook	$19.95	
	1-57248-122-6	Tenants' Rights in NY	$21.95	

NEW JERSEY TITLES

Qty	ISBN	Title	Retail	Ext.
	1-57248-239-7	How to File for Divorce in NJ	$24.95	

NORTH CAROLINA TITLES

Qty	ISBN	Title	Retail	Ext.
	1-57248-185-4	How to File for Divorce in NC (3E)	$22.95	
	1-57248-129-3	How to Make a NC Will (3E)	$16.95	
	1-57248-184-6	How to Start a Business in NC (3E)	$18.95	
	1-57248-091-2	Landlords' Rights & Duties in NC	$21.95	

OHIO TITLES

Qty	ISBN	Title	Retail	Ext.
	1-57248-190-0	How to File for Divorce in OH (2E)	$24.95	
	1-57248-174-9	How to Form a Corporation in OH	$24.95	
	1-57248-173-0	How to Make an OH Will	$16.95	

PENNSYLVANIA TITLES

Qty	ISBN	Title	Retail	Ext.
	1-57248-242-7	Child Custody, Visitation and Support in Pennsylvania	$26.95	
	1-57248-211-7	How to File for Divorce in PA (3E)	$26.95	
	1-57248-094-7	How to Make a PA Will (2E)	$16.95	
	1-57248-112-9	How to Start a Business in PA (2E)	$18.95	
	1-57248-245-1	The Landlord's Legal Guide in PA	$24.95	

TEXAS TITLES

Qty	ISBN	Title	Retail	Ext.
	1-57248-171-4	Child Custody, Visitation, and Support in TX	$22.95	
	1-57248-172-2	How to File for Divorce in TX (3E)	$24.95	
	1-57248-114-5	How to Form a Corporation in TX (2E)	$24.95	
	1-57248-255-9	How to Make a TX Will (3E)	$16.95	
	1-57248-214-1	How to Probate and Settle an Estate in TX (3E)	$26.95	
	1-57248-228-1	How to Start a Business in TX (3E)	$18.95	
	1-57248-111-0	How to Win in Small Claims Court in TX (2E)	$16.95	
	1-57248-110-2	Landlords' Rights and Duties in TX (2E)	$21.95	

SUBTOTAL THIS PAGE _____

SUBTOTAL PREVIOUS PAGE _____

Shipping — $5.00 for 1st book, $1.00 each additional _____

Illinois residents add 6.75% sales tax _____

Connecticut residents add 6.00% sales tax _____

TOTAL _____

To order, call Sourcebooks at 1-800-432-7444 or FAX (630) 961-2168 (Bookstores, libraries, wholesalers—please call for discount)
Prices are subject to change without notice.
Find more legal information at: www.SphinxLegal.com